PAPER DECORATIONS

PAPER DECORATIONS

Valerie Janitch

Photographs by Rob Matheson

PELHAM BOOKS

First published in Great Britain by
PELHAM BOOKS LTD
52 Bedford Square
London WC1B 3EF
1977

ISBN 0 7207 0978 4

Filmset in Great Britain by
Filmtype Services Ltd, Scarborough
Printed by Hollen Street Press Ltd at Slough, Berkshire
and bound by Dorstel Press Ltd at Harlow, Essex

CONTENTS

LIST OF COLOUR PLATES

INTRODUCTION

All through the year there are important events and anniversaries which call for a celebration. Well-chosen decorations will make them even more festive and memorable. There are the seasonal calendar occasions, such as Christmas, New Year, Easter and Hallowe'en; there are those traditional days when you remember someone special – Saint Valentine's, Mothering Sunday, Father's Day. And there are the personal family celebrations which happen at any time – birthdays, new babies, coming-of-age, engagements, weddings and anniversaries. And finally, there are those times when you want to wish someone good luck, bon voyage, congratulations, welcome home, a successful housewarming or a happy retirement.

You will find suitable designs for all these purposes in the following chapters, arranged in related groups. In many cases, a decoration from one section will need little or no alteration to adapt it for a different occasion. For instance, the daisy-chain bordered heart (p. 49) would make a charming Valentine. The Mother's and Father's Day bears (p. 17) might carry a different message to suit a variety of occasions. Old Father Owl (p. 19) would be just as appropriate for a masculine birthday, and the method of decorating Easter eggs (p. 16) could be used to make glamorous Christmas baubles to hang between the branches of the tree.

So when you want an idea for a decoration to mark a specific occasion, look first at the appropriate chapter, and then glance through the rest of the book and see what you and your imagination can produce.

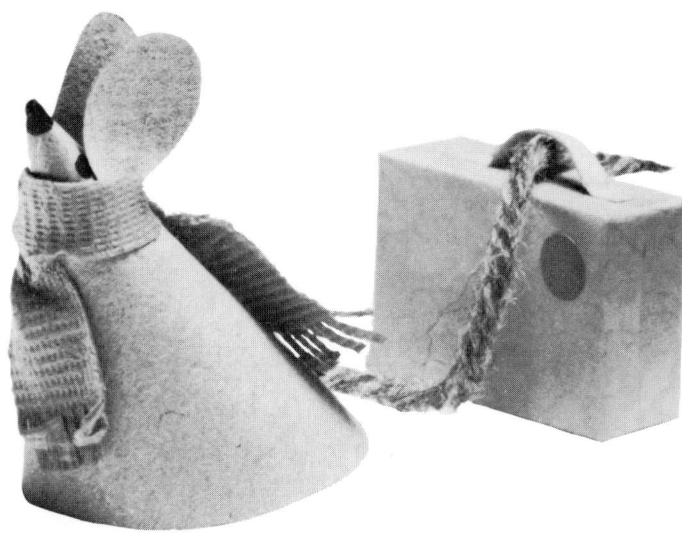

PAPER, TOOLS, EQUIPMENT AND TECHNIQUES

PAPERS TO USE

You will find many of the papers you need in your house already: face tissues, kitchen towels and their inner tubes, cake doilies, parcel wrapping, writing paper, gift-wrap, newspapers and magazines, wallpaper off-cuts, empty cartons (cornflakes, crispbreads, shirt boxes), manilla envelopes, cooking foil, all can be turned into exciting and professional looking decorations.

There are some papers you will need to buy – the most useful is 'cartridge' or 'construction' paper, which is fairly thick, and comes in a wide range of colours. The only disadvantage is that you have to buy a large sheet (about 20×30in – 50×75cm) which can make it expensive if you just want small pieces in several colours. You can overcome this problem with packets of (Wiggins Teape) 'Play Paper', which contain eighteen single sheets, about $12 \times 8\frac{1}{2}$in (30×22cm) each in a different colour (the range includes some particularly subtle shades, which can be very effective when matched together). You can also buy similar packets containing larger sheets of metallic 'Fun Paper', which are very useful when you want to make things in richly coloured foil. Tiny scraps of coloured paper can often be snipped from the illustrations in leaflets, catalogues and magazines.

You will find soft face tissues appearing over and over again in these decorations – they are so versatile and the attractively printed cartons often come in handy, too. Apart from plain white, you can buy large boxes of assorted colours, and Kleenex produce a variety of pretty smaller packs containing both pastel and deeper shades, like rose pink, lilac, violet, and a lovely clear cornflower-blue. Soft toilet paper can usually be substituted, and if you need a really strong colour, like red, brown or dark green, use soft table napkins. Notice that this kind of tissue has, in fact, two or three very thin layers – or 'plies' – and these can be separated if necessary.

Crêpe paper comes in a good range of artistic shades, and has the unique quality of stretching, which makes it ideal for realistic paper flowers with softly curved petals. Nevertheless, I have avoided using it in this book, as it comes in long lengths, so tends to become expensive if you want a number of colours.

Finally, it is not always practical to draw or paint round circles for eyes, noses, buttons, etc., and cutting them in paper can be rather fiddly (a hole punch is good for tiny circles). So use round self-adhesive labels, which can be bought in packets – black, white and assorted colours – and might have been made for the purpose.

ADHESIVES

For the majority of paper-sticking jobs, use a flexible latex adhesive: Copydex in a tube is good most of the time, although the jar is a great help for large areas. It is quick-acting and goes a long way so do not use too much – although any excess can be rubbed off with the fingertip. For non-porous surfaces, like metal, plastic or glass beads, and foil, use an all-purpose clear adhesive like Evo-stik or Bostik Stik 'n Fix, according to the specific job. To fix hanging decorations, use a small blob of Bostik Blu-tack.

Pasting and papier-mâché are cleanly and easily done with small quantities of Polycell wallpaper paste or Bostik Paper Paste. When dry, neither of these leaves a mark if you get them on the right side of your work. Only very small quantities of wallpaper paste are needed: allow about half a teaspoonful of powder from a sachet for a small decoration such as the basic mouse; increase the amount as needed. Mix with water in an old yoghourt or cream carton, following the directions on the packet, and adding more water if the paste is too thick.

Occasionally, you may not want to use a wet adhesive in case it damages your paper, or makes the colours run. A dry stick adhesive is the answer, such as Henkel's 'Pritt'.

Applying adhesives

A thick brush – about 1in (25mm) wide – is best for pasting. The Copydex tube comes with a little spatula for spreading, and the jar has a built-in brush. Evo-stik can be used direct from the long, narrow nozzle or on the head of a pin for very tiny amounts. Bostik Stik 'n Fix and Paper Paste both have their own trim-it brush. Simply draw the Pritt stick over the surface like a lipstick, but do not wind it up too far or it may snap off.

Adhesive tapes

For any taping job that is hidden, use ordinary clear Sellotape which has a shiny surface. But if the tape will show on the finished decoration, use Scotch magic transparent tape, which has a matt surface, making it almost invisible. And if you need something really strong for fixing, Sellotape's coloured cloth tape is very reliable.

TOOLS AND EQUIPMENT

Only a few are essential and these will usually be found around the house.

Large scissors
Small scissors, preferably pointed embroidery type
Ruler, with metal edge if possible
Compasses
Sharp pencil (a Pentel saves continual sharpening)
Eraser
Craft knife (the Olfa with 'snap-off' blades is efficient)
Blunt knife for scoring
Fine steel knitting needle
Black and brown fibre-tip pens (eg Tempo range)

Also helpful are:

Set square and protractor
Hole punch and mini-stapler
Manicure or cocktail sticks
Paper clips and pins
Fine wire and sewing thread
Graph paper and ordinary greaseproof paper for tracing
Thin card for making templates (patterns)
Plasticine (Harbutt's) for weighting decorations if necessary

For colouring the decorations:

Reeves poster paints
Waterproof drawing inks
Tempo felt markers

MEASURING

All the instructions for making the decorations are given in both Imperial and Metric measures. Do not compare the measurements, as the conversions are seldom accurate, they may even differ: $\frac{1}{2}$in might be interpreted as 10mm here and 15mm there. This is because the metric equivalent given is always the nearest *practical* measurement which is most suitable, in each

specific instance. This makes measuring easy on
either kind of ruler and ensures that the finished
result is perfectly in proportion.

Circles

When measuring circles remember:
>   the *diameter* is the distance across the centre
>   from one side of the circle to the other
>   the *radius* is the distance between compass
>   points from the centre to the edge (half the
>   diameter)
>   the *circumference* is the distance all round the
>   edge of the circle.

BEGINNING WITH A MOUSE

The basic mouse appears in a different costume in every colour plate.

This little mouse runs right through the book in a variety of roles and costumes, showing how easy it is to adapt a decoration for different occasions.

The basic design for the mouse, as pictured, is very simple. Making it is a good way to get the feel of working with paper, and to experiment with some of the techniques you will meet repeatedly in the following pages.

Directions for the various mouse disguises are included in the relevant sections.

Materials

Paper – medium weight paper of almost any kind, in any colour. The one in the picture was made from the inside of an old manilla envelope. The pages of scrap-books often provide subtle mouse-greys and soft muddy browns; or you could use a bright green or pinky-mauve paper to make a psychedelic mouse.

Scrap of pink face tissue

Short length of wool, yarn or string, to match the paper

Black ink, paint or a fibre-tip pen, to mark features

Strong quick-drying adhesive (such as Copydex) to stick ears

Method:

1. Fold a piece of tracing paper in half and trace the pattern (Fig. 1), placing the folded edge exactly level with the line indicated. Add all the markings – including the half-circle for the tail. Now turn the folded paper over and trace your original tracing through on to the other half. Open out the paper and you will have a full-size pattern.

Fig. 1

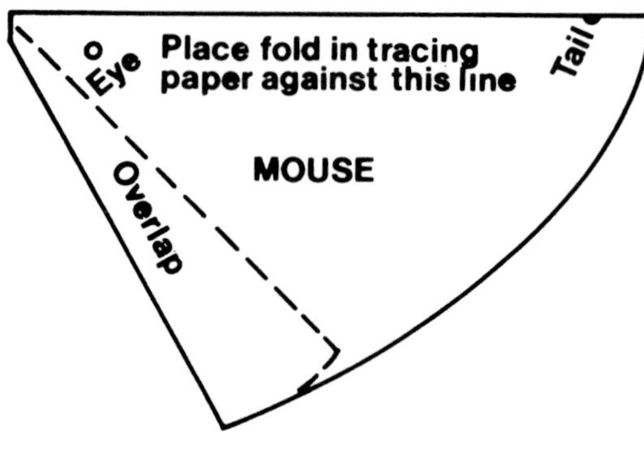

2. Transfer the tracing to a piece of thin card (basic methods 1 and 2 – p. 66), to make a sturdy template which you can keep to use over and over again. Cut out carefully, and punch small holes for the eyes and tail.

3. Place the template on your paper and, holding it firmly down to prevent any movement, draw round it. Mark circles for the eyes and tail.

14

The basic mouse in all its different outfits

4. Cut out. Punch a small hole for the tail.
5. Brush paste liberally *all over* the wrong side of the paper (this will make it curve round smoothly, and also stiffen the paper when it is dry). Curve round into a cone shape and stick the straight edges together, overlapping as indicated. Leave to dry.
6. Trace the ear pattern and make a template. Cut twice in mouse paper – *reversing the pattern for the second ear*.
7. Separate the two plies of the face tissue, and paste one layer only to the inside of each ear. When dry, trim tissue level.
8. Mark the eyes and nose in black, following the illustration and markings.
9. Stick the ears into position as shown, with a little adhesive below the broken line.
10. Cut a short length of wool, yarn or string for the tail. Thread through the hole then knot end inside to hold. Smear a little Copydex on the cut end and roll between the fingertips to prevent fraying.

FAMILY OCCASIONS

These decorations are illustrated in colour plate 1 facing page 20

Some decorative ideas to take the place of a greetings card.

FLOWERY EASTER EGGS

In the days of the Tsars, it was an Easter custom at the Russian court to give fabulous eggs – often made of gold and richly decorated with priceless jewels. Naturally, they were treasured and proudly displayed long after Easter . . . as yours will be, if you make these colourful eggs studded with flowers.

Materials

Eggs (blown – as below)
Coloured face tissues (or paper napkins)
Coloured paper, doilies, gift-wrap, tiny seed
   pearls and beads, to trim
Wallpaper paste
Copydex adhesive

1. Using a darning needle, carefully bore a small hole at the pointed end of the egg. Make a larger hole at the broad end. Stir the needle around inside, to break the yolk. Hold egg over a bowl: place mouth against pointed end and blow steadily. Wash empty shell in warm water, and dry gently.
2. Separate the two layers of a face tissue. Cut one into sixteen equal pieces.
3. Coat surface of egg with a thick layer of paste. Then cover with overlapping squares of tissue, gently smoothing into place. Add more paste (with fingertips), and the remaining squares, followed by a final layer of paste.
4. Leave on a piece of foil in a warm place until absolutely dry.

Decorating your egg

The possibilities are endless – but plate 1 (facing p. 20), may give you some ideas. The *blue* one has tiny white flowers cut from a paper doily; a spiral of flowers cut from gift-wrap is pasted round the *violet* egg. 'Forget-me-not' clusters on the *white* egg are papier-mâché rosettes (basic method 16 – p. 71) made from 1in (25mm) squares of blue tissue, set in similar rosettes made from $1\frac{1}{4}$in (30mm) squares of green tissue. The *pale green* egg is divided into quarters with narrow strips of darker green paper cut with pinking shears; the tiny papier mâché flowers (basic method 18 – p. 71) are made from $\frac{1}{2}$in (15mm) squares of deep yellow tissue, set on green paper leaves. The *pink* and *lilac* eggs are both decorated with pearl-centred papier-mâché flowers and green leaves. The *lime green* egg has brown papier-mâché flowers, set off by tiny gilt and green glass beads and crowned by a large pearl.

Stands

Thread a few tiny beads or pearls on cotton and tie in a circle. Stick egg firmly on top.

PUFFY EASTER CHICKS

Have your newly-hatched chicks struggling out

of broken egg-shells. Or stick them to a egg-shaped base: those illustrated (facing p. 20) were cut from the patterned side of the box which contained the tissues – using the perforated oval removed from the top of the carton as a template.

Materials

Yellow face tissues
Orange paper for beak and feet
Black paper (or adhesive labels) for eyes
Copydex adhesive

1. Make a puff-ball, following basic method 14 (p. 70): use circles E–F–G–H–I–J–K for each half – but do not stick halves together.
2. For each wing, cut another circle I: then cut in half. Staple together at one corner. Stick stapled ends of wings to one half of puff-ball – as Fig. 2. Stick other half of ball on top.

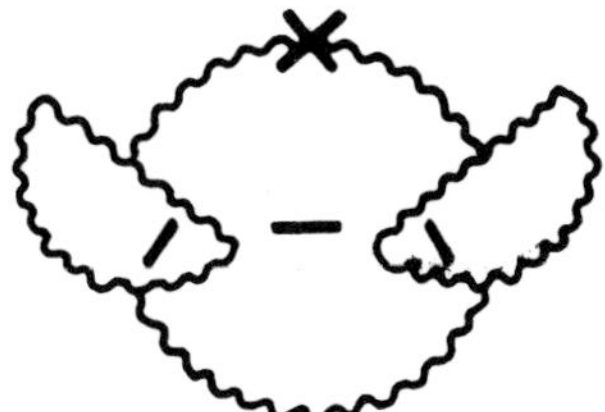

Fig. 2

3. Cut one circle each I–J–K for the tail. Stick together at the centre – but keep flat – with all the staples in the same direction. Dab adhesive at centre of top circle (K), and fold in half. Separate puff-ball slightly at *x*: insert adhesive then push tail between layers and press firmly together.
4. Trace beak on to orange paper (basic method 1 – p. 66). Cut out, score broken line and fold in half. Smear adhesive along back of fold, then push between layers of tissue at front.
5. Trace feet on to folded orange paper. Cut, open out and stick back section under body.

Fig. 3

6. Cut the eyes in black paper (or use labels), and stick at each side of beak, as illustrated.

FATHER'S AND MOTHER'S DAY BEARS

These animated bears, waving their cheerful banners, are easily adapted. Just change the message to suit the event, and they will carry your greeting on almost any happy occasion.

Materials

Golden-brown paper } or golden-brown
Thin card } card
White or coloured paper for banners
2 wooden toothpicks or cocktail sticks
4 small 2-pronged paper fasteners
Strong thread or fine crochet cotton
Adhesive tape
Wallpaper paste (optional)
Copydex adhesive
Evo-stik clear adhesive

Father
Red paper for waistcoat
Tiny gilt beads for buttons
Plastic-covered (insulating) wire for pipe
Small round wooden bead for pipe

Mother
Flowery gift-wrap paper (or alternative) for
  dress, hat and decoration

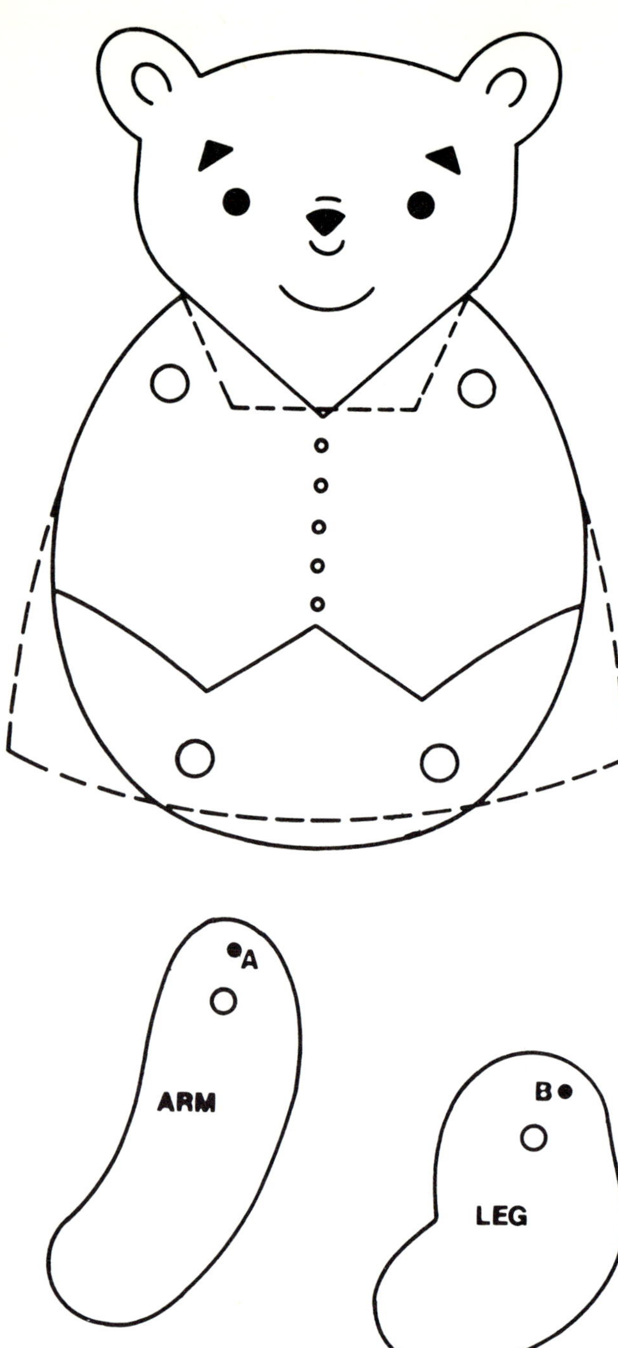

Fig. 4

18

Father

1. Paste golden-brown paper to card. When dry, trace the body once as Fig. 4, and the arm and leg twice each, on to card (basic method 1 – p. 66) *reversing pattern for second arm and leg* (ignore broken lines). Cut out.
2. Trace waistcoat only on to red paper. Cut out and paste to body. Stick beads down centre for buttons.
3. Assemble and string puppet as basic method 10 – p. 68.
4. Draw features in brown and black (or black only).
5. Cut a 1½in (4cm) length of wire. Bend up ¼in (5mm) at one end and cut away ¼in (5mm) of plastic at the other (see Fig. 5). Push bare wire through card at side of mouth: bend over and fix securely behind with tape. Stick wooden bead on up-turned end, for bowl of pipe.

Fig. 5

6. Make banners from thin white card: cut *two* pieces 1¾ × ¾in (4 × 2cm) – width × depth, and stick together to make a double thickness (for correct balance) – and cut *one* piece 2 × 1¼in (5 × 3cm) width × depth.
7. Write message on banners, then with Evo-stick, attach one end of a toothpick behind each banner and the other end to the front of paw.

Mother

1. As Father – but ignore waistcoat and *follow broken lines* for lower part of body and neckline of dress.
2. Cut dress in gift-wrap, and paste to body. Draw lacy edge round neckline. Cut out single flowers from gift-wrap paper and stick to head for her hat, as illustrated (facing p. 20).

3. Assemble and string puppet as basic method 10 – p. 68.
4. Draw features in brown and black (or black only).
5. Paste coloured paper to card for banners: trace heart shape and draw a circle 1¾in (45 mm) in diameter. Cut out.

Fig. 6

6. As Father 7 – adding tiny cut-out flower shapes for decoration.

OLD FATHER OWL

A square owl peers out of the square hole in a square tree, making an amusing decoration for Father's Day, and there is room in the tree for a small gift.

Materials

Thin card
Brown paper for owl, with scraps of yellow, bright orange, deep orange, black and white
White face tissues
Poster paints
Green paper for leaves
Wallpaper paste
Copydex adhesive

Tree

1. Cut card 13 × 8in (32.5 × 20cm) – width ×

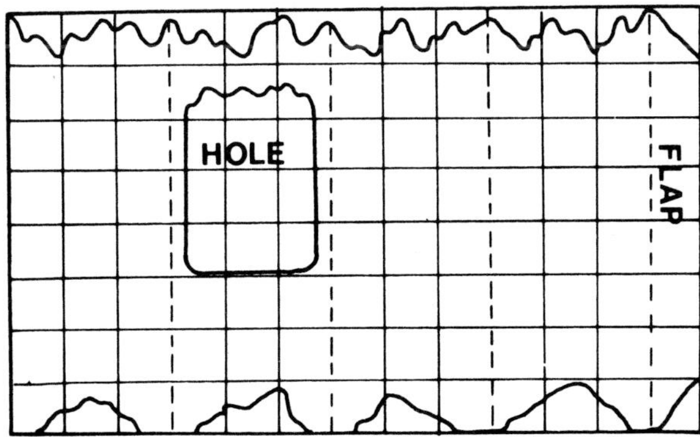

Fig. 7

depth, and rule into 1in (25mm) squares, as Fig. 7. Mark four vertical broken lines, and score.
2. Cut jagged edge of broken bark at top, and areas between 'roots' at bottom – but leave at least 1in (25mm) of straight lower edge remaining at base of each scored line, and ½in (15mm) at the corner (see Fig. 7).
3. Cut out hole, as indicated.
4. Paint the back with black poster colour.
5. When dry, bend round into shape, and stick flap inside.
6. To make bark, tear a face tissue into four long strips. Brush one strip very generously with paste, leaving about ½in (15mm) unpasted at ends for lifting. Place strip flat on card – ends overlapping top and bottom. Push the wet tissue sideways, gathering it into wrinkles to cover about ½in (13mm). Continue to add more strips, making the surface rough and uneven like a gnarled old tree trunk: use shorter strips above and below hole.
7. Leave about ⅜in (10mm) overlapping edges of card – but trim level along *straight* lower edge at each corner, and lower edge of hole. Paste overlap and turn neatly over to back of card. Leave to dry.
8. Add dark brown to a wash (very liquid paint mixture) of mid-grey poster colour, and paint bark thickly with two or three coats. Paint overlapping tissue inside, black.

Owl

1. Cut brown paper $3\frac{3}{4} \times 7$in (9.5×17cm) and paste to card. When dry, trim card level. Score vertical broken lines as Fig. 8.

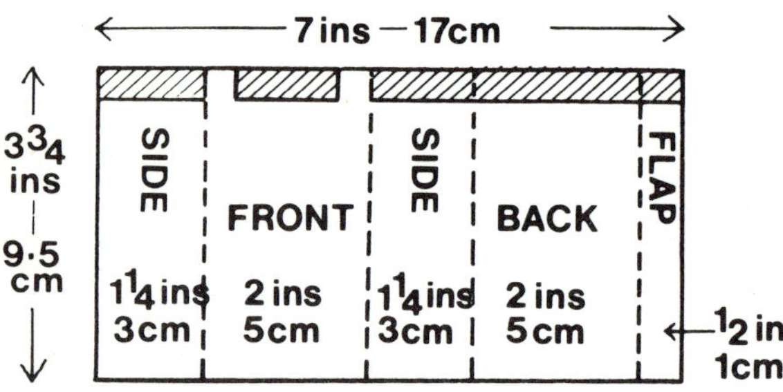

Fig. 8

2. Trace the owl (Fig. 9) on to front section (basic method 1 – p. 66). Cut away section between ears – and the equivalent depth along sides and back, as shaded areas on Fig. 8. Cut slits at each side of feet.

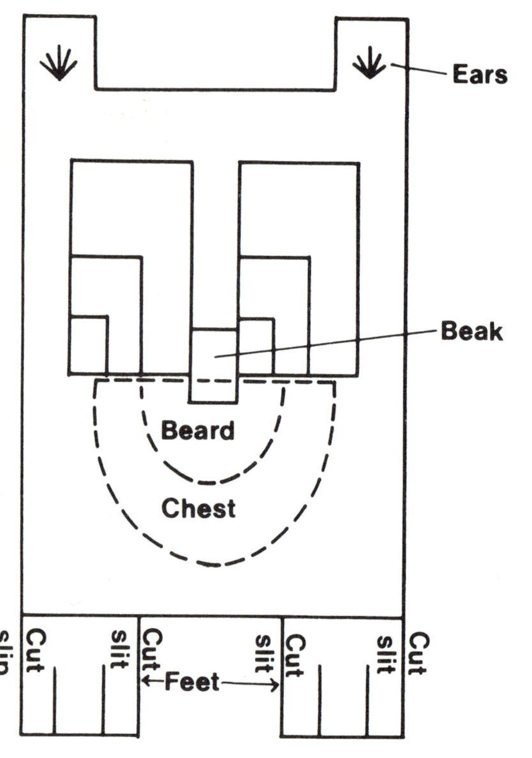

Fig. 9

3. Trace the *whole* of each eye on to white paper: outline in black and cut out. Trace the inner eye – including pupil – on to yellow paper: outline in black, cut out and stick to outer eye. Trace the pupil on to black paper: cut out and stick in place. Stick eyes into position.

4. Trace patterns for chest and beard, following broken lines. Fold face tissue in half: place straight edge of chest pattern against fold and cut curve with pinking shears. Cut beard the same. Stick beard lightly to chest at top and centre. Then stick chest to body.

5. Cut beak in bright orange: outline in black and stick into place.

6. Cut feet in deep orange: outline in black and stick into place.

7. Mark ears in black, as pattern.

8. Bend round into shape and stick flap inside.

9. Cut separate top of head in brown paper, Fig. 10. Slit sides of ears, as indicated. Score broken lines. Snip a fine fringe along lower half of flap between ears, as indicated – and *also* along lower edge of the sides and back. Bend the ears up and fringed flaps down.

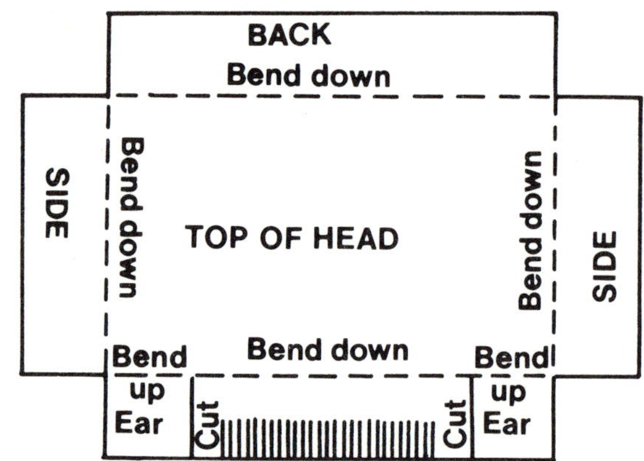

Fig. 10

10. Place top of head on owl, fringe overlapping all round. Stick backs of ears together. Stick the upper, un-fringed, half of the flaps round top of head.

Plate 1: Old Father Owl: Father's and Mother's Day Bears: Easter eggs and chicks: Easter bonnet mouse

Plate 2: clockwise from top: **Fairy Silver Wings**: Rabbit: Stork: Panda: Kitten: Puppy: Baby mouse
and Nurse: Lion: Sleeping Beauty cradle

Plate 3: Fruit-cake fort: Totem pole: Redskin mice: Regimental band

11. Cut the wing twice in brown paper. Snip fringe round curved edge, as indicated. Spread

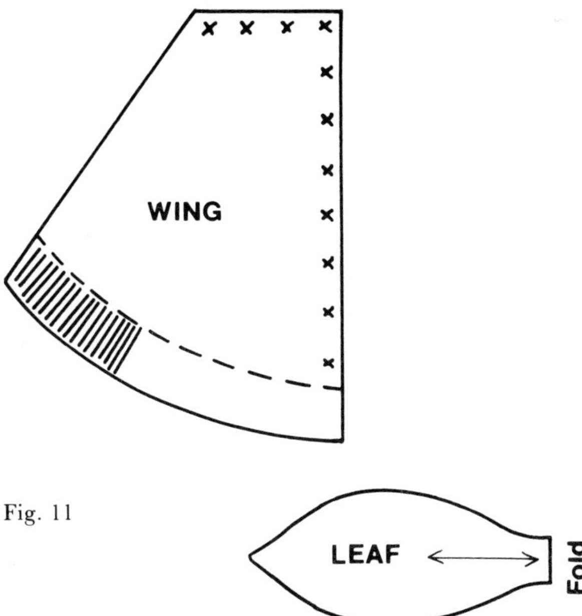

Fig. 11

adhesive along top and back edges   as *x*'s – then stick to side of body, level with back edge, and $\frac{5}{8}$in (15mm) below top of head.

To assemble

1. Fit owl inside tree: push feet outside, over lower edge of hole, and press down firmly.
2. Cut four pairs of leaves in folded green paper. Open out and stick two pairs together at the centre: twist over and stick to side of tree, as illustrated (facing p. 20). Repeat for front spray.

EASTER BONNET MOUSE

Make the mouse as directed on p. 14. Her bonnet is a semicircle of paper doily, backed and trimmed with deep violet tissue paper. A blue face tissue flower sits between her ears, and another under her chin (basic method 15 – p. 71).

Plate 4 opposite: Snow maidens mobile: Snow Queen's castle: Emily-Kate: Fairy mouse

---

BABIES AND EARLY BIRTHDAYS

These decorations are illustrated in colour plate 2 between pages 20–21

A special decoration is a charming way to announce the arrival of a new baby, to celebrate a Christening or a first birthday.

SEPTIMUS STORK

To welcome a new baby or stand guard over the Christening cake – Septimus is made from puff-balls, like the Easter chicks. He stands firmly on a piece of flower-printed card cut from the box containing the tissues which made him: and if you touch his beak, he will rock back and forth, nodding his head.

Materials

White face tissues
Golden-yellow face tissue or napkin for legs
Golden-yellow paper for feet
Golden-brown paper for beak
Black paper (or adhesive labels) for eyes
Stiff card (from tissue box) for base
2 pipe-cleaners
Copydex adhesive

1. Make a puff-ball for the head (basic method 14 – p. 70): cut circles G–H–I–K for each half but do not stick the halves together.
2. Make another puff-ball for the body, using circles A–B–C–D–E–G for each half but do not stick the halves together.
3. Bend a pipe-cleaner in half for his neck, and bind with white tissue (basic method 4 – p. 66): curve into an 's' shape (see Fig. 12).
4. Trace the beak on to folded golden-brown paper (basic method 1 – p. 66): cut out. Stick

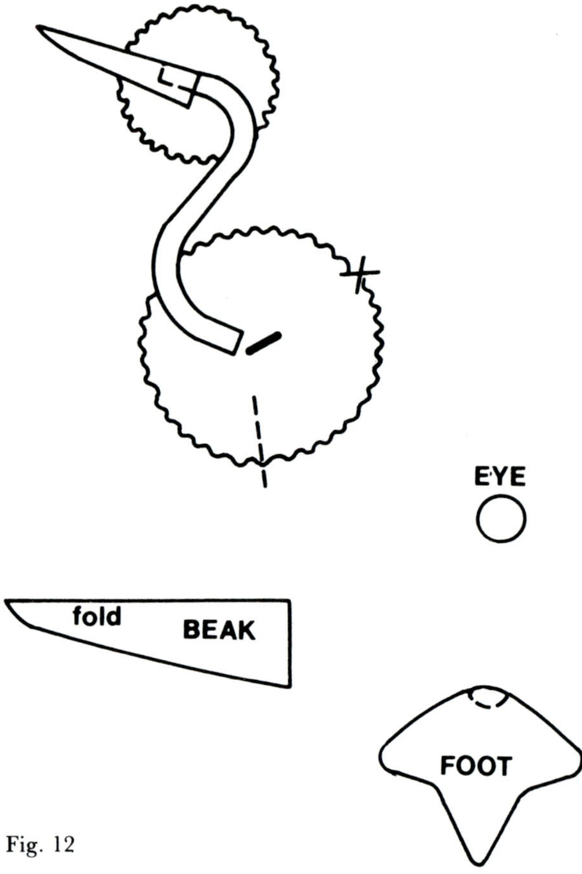

Fig. 12

the top $\frac{1}{4}$in (5mm) of the neck inside the broad end of the beak, fold on top (see Fig. 12).
5. Stick the top of the neck and beak across the back of one half of the head and stick the bottom end of the neck to the back of one body half – position as shown.

6. Stick the remaining halves of the head and body into place.

7. Cut a pipe-cleaner in half for the legs. Bind each with golden-yellow. Divide the tissues underneath the body, between circles B and C at each side, and stick the top of each leg between the layers – position as broken line in Fig. 12.

8. Cut each foot in *double* paper. Bend the bottom $\frac{3}{8}$in (10mm) of each leg up and stick between the two foot pieces, cutting the top piece as broken line.

9. Bend the legs slightly, as shown between pp. 20–21, and stick the feet firmly to a piece of card.

10. Make a half puff-ball for the tail, using circles F–G–H. Stick to the body at *x*.

11. Cut the eyes in black (or use labels) and stick at each side of head, as illustrated.

SLEEPING BEAUTY CRADLE

A dreamy, fairytale cradle to celebrate the arrival of a new baby or decorate the Christening cake. The one shown (between pp. 20–21) is lilac, with violet flowers trimming the hood. But any pastel colour will do: blue for a boy, pink for a girl – yellow if the baby is not born yet. Or a white cradle, with pink or blue flowers and matching pillow and coverlet.

Materials

Lilac face tissues (or alternative)
Violet face tissues (for flower trim)
Paper doily to trim
Thin card
Stiff paper (or *very* thin card)
Matchbox
Flat lollipop stick
Pipe-cleaner
Cotton wool
Adhesive tape
Wallpaper paste
Copydex adhesive

1. Cut two ovals of thin card as follows: draw a 2in (5cm) line A–B and, with centre A, draw a 2in (5cm) diameter circle. Repeat with centre B. Join C–D at each side, parallel to A–B (see Fig. 13).

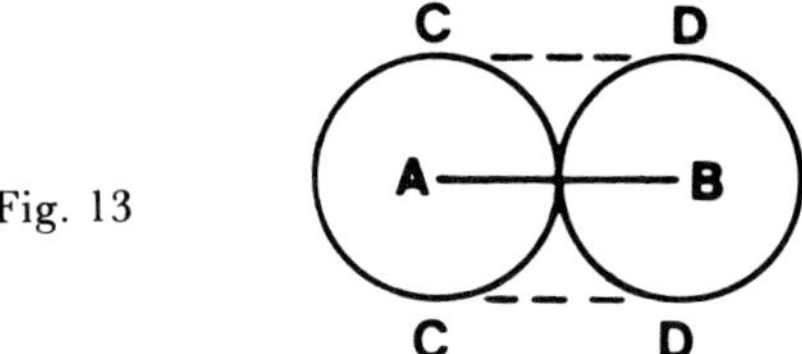

Fig. 13

2. Stick one oval on top of the matchbox outer cover and one beneath. Stick the drawer of the matchbox upside-down underneath the bottom oval.

3. Cut a strip of stiff paper 2×12in (5×30cm) – depth × length. Wrap this round the oval foundation so that the lower edge is level with the bottom of the matchbox drawer: overlap at one end – and *tape* the join.

4. Cut pieces of tissue 3in (7cm) deep, with a scalloped lower edge (basic method 9 – p. 68), and drape round the sides – folding over the top edge and sticking inside.

5. Stick sections of doily round as illustrated (snip down between motifs for a smooth fit).

6. Repeat 4 – with pieces 2in (5cm) deep, draping only about $\frac{1}{2}$in (10mm) over on the outside, to cover top of doily.

7. Shape the middle of a pipe-cleaner round

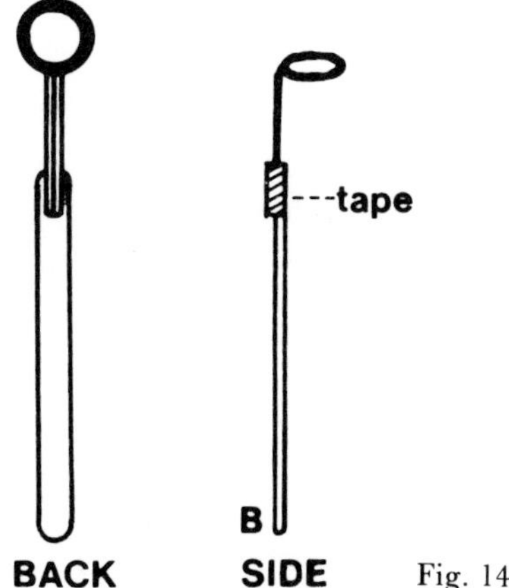

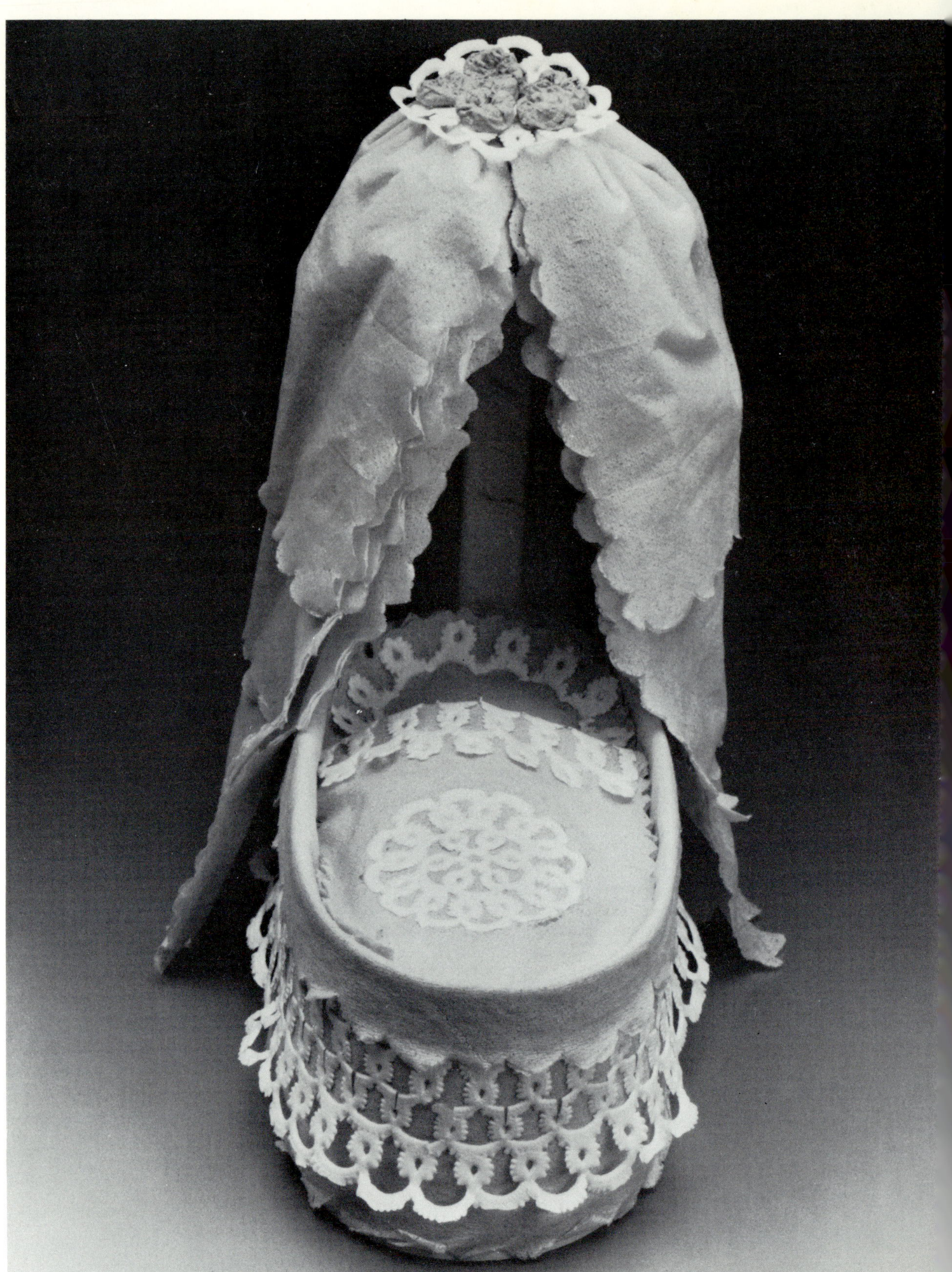

into a $\frac{3}{4}$in (2cm) diameter circle: then tape the ends to the top of a lollipop stick as Fig. 14 – to measure $6\frac{1}{4}$in (16cm) in all. Bend the circle over at right angles as shown (Fig. 14), and bind between A–B with tissue (basic method 4 – p. 66).

8. Slit the tissue along the top edge of the cradle at the head end where card joined, and push the lolly stick down between the overlap.

9. Pad the inside with cotton wool. Make a pattern as Fig. 13, and cut several layers of tissue together – preferably with pinking shears – slightly larger. Edge head end with scraps of doily for pillow effect, and place inside cradle.

10. Cut a similar piece for the coverlet – and fold one end under, $1\frac{1}{4}$in (3cm) from the top. Stick doily 'sheet' over folded edge, and trim centre with a lacy motif. Tuck inside cradle.

11. To make the hood, cut a scalloped edge along three sides of *three* 8in (20cm) square tissues. Place one over another, straight edges at the top and sides level – the lower edge of each tissue $1\frac{1}{2}$in (4cm) above the one below (Fig. 15). Pin together at the top, as indicated, and run a gathering thread across, $6\frac{1}{2}$in (16.5 cm) above the lower edge. Cut away surplus $\frac{1}{2}$in (15mm) above the gathers.

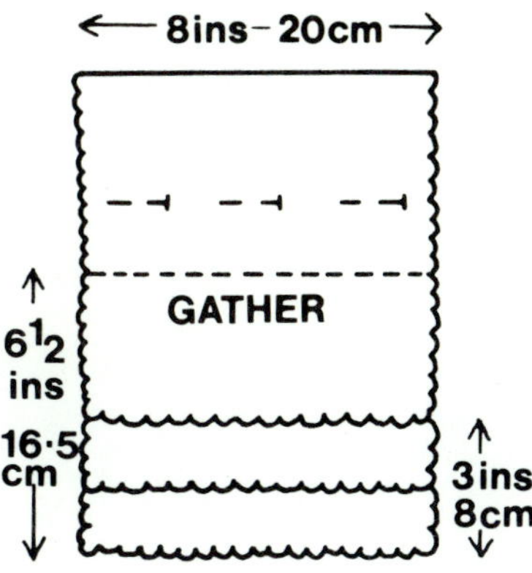

Fig. 15

Sleeping Beauty cradle

12. Draw up gathers and secure. Then push the gathered edge down through the pipe-cleaner circle, and arrange hood neatly round head of cradle, sticking lightly inside.

13. Make five papier-mâché flowers (basic method 18 – p. 71), using *two* 1in (25mm) squares of violet tissue. Cut out a doily motif and stick the flowers to it in a circle. Stick on top of hood.

FAIRY SILVER-WINGS

A fairy to hang over the cradle at a Christening or over the cake at a birthday party, bestowing good wishes on all the guests, her dress perhaps echoing the colour of the icing.

Materials

White and blue face tissues (or alternative) for dress
Flesh pink face tissue
Brown table napkin or golden-yellow face tissue for hair
White doily for skirt
Silver doily for wings (or silver paper or kitchen foil)
White paper for wings
1in (25mm) diameter pressed cotton ball available from craft shops (see stockists p. 73) or use flesh-coloured Plasticine
3 pipe-cleaners
Flesh-coloured poster paint
Flesh-coloured and black or white sewing thread
Tiny seed pearls or beads, to trim hair
Tiny pin (optional)
Toothpick or fine dried grass stem, for wand
Silver stars for wand (optional)
Wallpaper paste
Copydex adhesive
Evo-stik clear adhesive

1. Paint the head (on a matchstick) and leave to dry.

2. Bend a pipe-cleaner in half for the body:
bind 1in (25mm) at the bent end with pink
tissue.
3. Bend two more pipe-cleaners in half, and
make into single arms (basic method 11 – p. 69).
4. Bend the top of each arm down at right
angles 2in (5cm) from the tip of the hand.
5. Fit (but do not fix) the head over the bound
end of the body: place an arm at each side (see
Fig. 16), and bind tightly together with thread.
Remove head.

Fig. 16

6. Using pinking shears for the curved edge,
cut a 4in (10cm) diameter semi-circle of white
tissue for each sleeve. Fold into a quarter-circle,
then curve round into a cone shape, overlapping
and sticking the straight edges, fold on top.
7. Cut $\frac{1}{4}$in (6–7mm) off the tip of each sleeve,
and slit the join below another $\frac{1}{4}$in (6–7mm).
Fit sleeves over arms, join underneath, and
stick top corners to body.
8. Cut a strip of white tissue $8 \times \frac{1}{2}$in (20cm ×
10mm) length × width. Stick one end to the
body, close under an arm, and bind tightly
round: take the strip over one shoulder, round
the body twice more, then over the other
shoulder, finishing round the body again.
Stick the end down neatly.
9. Place three blue tissues on top of each other
for the skirt, and cut a 6in (15cm) diameter
circle with pinking shears. Separate into six
single layers. One by one, gather the centre of
each circle to form a point, and stick to sur-
round the waist.
10. Cut a section of white doily about $2–2\frac{1}{2}$in
(5–6cm) deep, and 9–10in (23–25cm) round
the outer edge. Fit round over skirt and stick

join at back. Then gather and stick the top
edge evenly round the waist. Finally, bind
waist with a folded strip of white tissue with
join at back.
11. Stick a scrap of doily round neck for collar,
as illustrated.
12. Cut the wings in folded white paper. Open
out and paste to the back of a silver doily (or
silver paper or kitchen foil). Trim doily level
with paper shape – then repeat for other side.
When dry, refold at centre and stick fold to
back of figure, reinforcing with a tiny pin.

Fig. 17

13. Replace head on matchstick, and make the
hairstyle as basic method 12 – p. 69, following
the illustration for guidance.
14. When dry, fix head in position. Stick loops
of pearls at each side, and trim with papier
mâché flowers (basic method 18 – p. 71), made
from 1in (25mm) squares of blue tissue – and
tiny silver leaves cut from doily or kitchen foil.
15. Curve the figure round into flying position.
Pass a length of thread (about 24in (60cm) – or
length required) through the hair on the crown
of the head: then thread each end separately
through the back of the skirt – halfway down
and about $1\frac{1}{2}$in (4cm) apart. Divide the two
ends of the body pipe-cleaner beneath the skirt
to form legs and tie one end of the thread to
each. Control balance by adjusting position of
pipe-cleaners.
16. Stick silver stars to end of toothpick, and
stick to hand.
17. Mark round dots for eyes as basic method
13 – p. 70.

Fairy Silver-Wings

BIRTHDAY ANIMALS

Very young children love baby animals: here is a basic pattern which can be adapted to make Ming-ho the panda, Violet Kitten, Lancelot Lion, Theodore Bear, Rosie Rabbit and Pudding the puppy. Stand them around the cake – or in a small group on top.

Materials

Face tissues or paper napkins for heads
Medium-weight paper for bodies, ears, legs and arms
Scraps of black and coloured paper (or adhesive labels) for features
Pipe-cleaner (or matchstick)
Wool, yarn or string for tails (except rabbit)
Adhesive tape
Wallpaper paste (optional)
Copydex adhesive

1. Make a puff-ball for the head (basic method 14 – p. 70). For the back half, use circles E–F–G–H–I–K: but for the front half, omit E, and use only F–G–H–I–K. Do not stick together.
2. Draw a 4½in (11cm) diameter semi-circle for the body, as Fig. 18. *Without adjusting your compasses*, place the point at B and mark C. With centre A again, draw a 1½in (35mm) semi-circle. Join A–C to mark overlap. Cut out as indicated.

Fig. 18

3. Curve round into a cone (as mouse – p. 14) and stick overlap.

28

4. Stick one end of a 2in (5cm) length of pipe-cleaner (or a matchstick) to the flat back of the smaller half puff-ball (front of head) – for the neck.
5. Trace the ears on to coloured paper (basic method 1 – p. 66), reversing pattern for second ear, and cut out. For all animals except puppy, hold the neck and stick the base of each ear to the flat back of the puff-ball (checking correct position from the front).
6. For the *lion only*, cut one puff-ball circle A in golden-brown. Snip about ¼in (5mm) between each notch to make his fringed mane. Stick behind the half ball as illustrated.
7. Stick the two halves of the ball together. Then lower the pipe-cleaner down into the body cone and fix at the front with tape.
8. Cut the eyes, noses, tongues and paws in coloured paper (or use labels): stick into position, as shown (between pp. 20–21). Add puppy's ears.

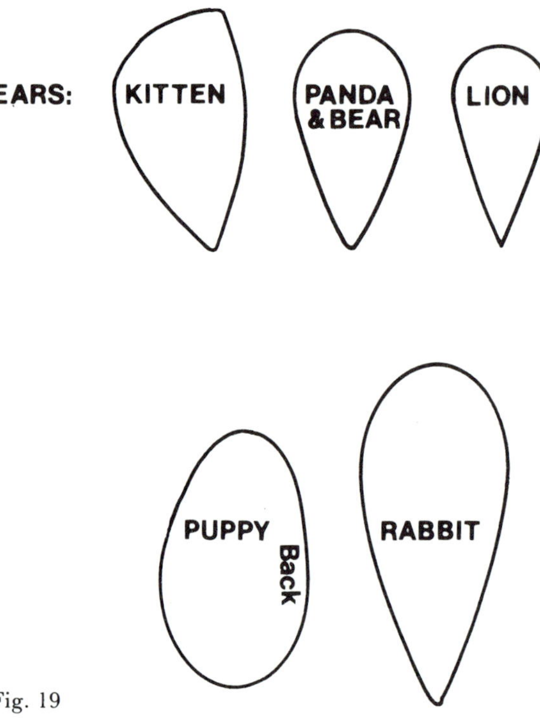

Fig. 19

Fig. 20

9. For all animals except rabbit, punch a small hole at the back, near the base, and knot wool, yarn or string through for the tail (as for mouse – p. 14).

For the rabbit's tail, make a half puff-ball in white tissue, using circles K–L–M. Stick into place.

NURSE-MOUSE AND BABY

The basic mouse (p. 14) wears a cap and apron cut from a paper doily.

Cut a 1in (25mm) diameter semi-circle for the baby's head: paste into a cone as for the mouse. When dry, mark the eyes and nose. Cut the ears as Fig. 21 (ignore broken lines) in the same paper.

Fill a walnut shell with cotton wool. Stick the ears at the 'pillow' end – then stick the head on top, as indicated by the broken line. Tuck more cotton wool on top, if necessary. A tiny lump of Plasticine underneath keeps the cradle steady.

Fig. 21 

MR MANY HAPPY RETURNS

These decorations are illustrated in colour plate 3 between pages 20–21

The best birthday party decorations reflect the interests of the person concerned, and their guests. Here are some ideas with a masculine theme for a little boy's birthday party.

FORT FRUIT-CAKE

The walls and towers of this fort can be made of crispbread and cornflakes packets, or any cartons of roughly the same proportions.

For a more solid building after the party, stick the ends of the walls to the towers, and mount the whole thing on a firm base – a square papier-mâché cake stand would be ideal.

Materials

4 cardboard cartons for walls – about 7 × 4 × 1½in
   (18 × 10 × 4cm) – width × height × depth
2 cereal packets for towers – about 8½ × 12 × 3in
   (22 × 30 × 8cm) – width × height × depth
Wall or shelf lining paper
Mid and dark grey paper for archway and
   entrance
Black paper for windows
Brown (wood-grain if possible) paper for
   drawbridge
Coloured paper for flags
Stiff card for drawbridge
String for drawbridge
4 drinking straws for flagpoles
4 large, 4 medium and 4 tiny beads for
   flagpoles
4 pins – at least 1in (25mm) long
Plasticine

Light grey poster paint
Mid grey oil pastel crayon or alternative
Adhesive tape
Wallpaper paste
Copydex adhesive
Evo-stik clear adhesive

Walls

1. Measure and mark battlements on front of box, as Fig. 22: *these* are ¾in (20mm) deep and 1in (25mm) wide.

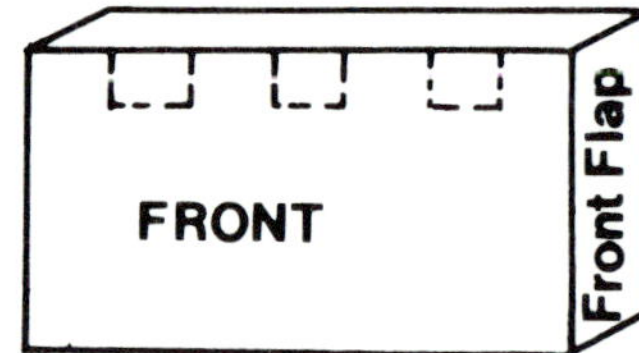

Fig. 22

2. Rule a horizontal line on the *back* of the box, the same depth as the front battlements (¾in – 20mm).

3. Open out flaps and flatten box. Cut round the front battlements, and along the horizontal line on the back – continuing across the flaps, keeping in one piece.

4. Turn over the section you have just *cut away* (Fig. 23), and cut the short flaps off the back. Stick the printed side of the portion which was originally the back of the box, behind the front battlements (shaded section in Fig. 24): cut out to match the battlements.

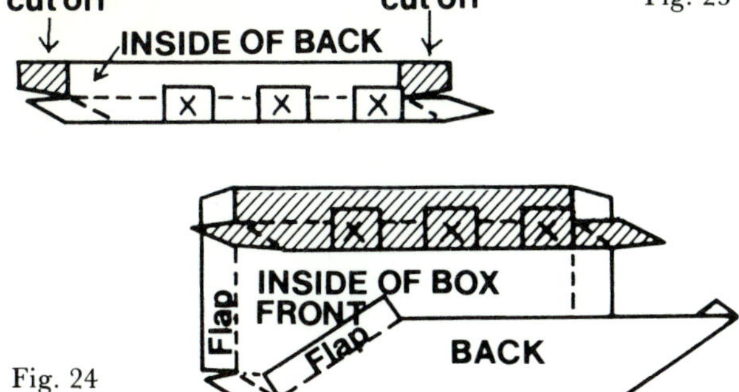

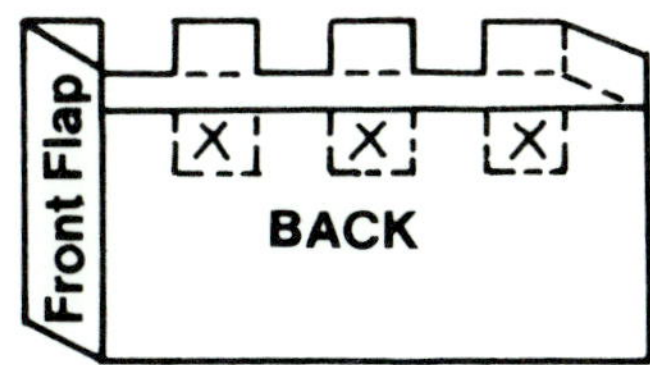

Fig. 24

5. Fold box back into shape. Turn down the tabs marked *x*, tuck inside and stick to the back (Fig. 25). Finally, fold down short flaps at each end and stick the long ones over them (something firm pushed inside before sealing up will support the sides later: I used two toilet roll inners).

Fig. 25

6. Paste lining paper all over the box, folding it smoothly round; mitre battlement corners (basic method 3, p. 66).

Towers

1. Cut cereal packet completely in half, as vertical broken line, Fig. 26.

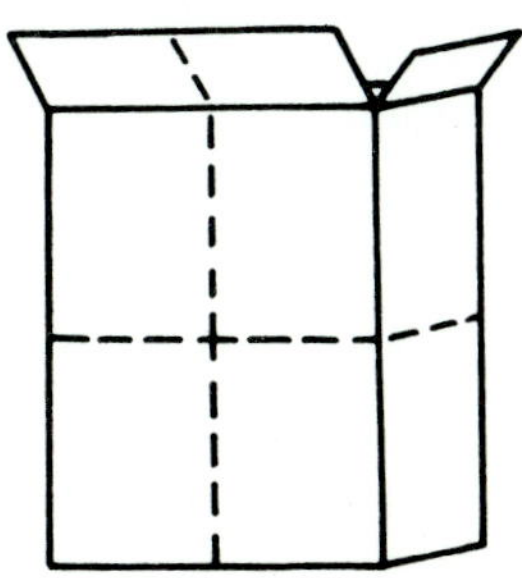

Fig. 26

2. Cut away the top half of each section (horizontal broken line – Fig. 26), leaving the lower part the height you want your tower to be: the one illustrated is 6in (15cm).

3. On the back and front, measure and score a vertical line to make them the same width as the side – see Fig. 27 where B = A (3in – 8cm – here). Cut each side of the base below C (*x–x*) to the scored line, then score the base to correspond, and bend up. Bend pieces C round and stick over base flap (Fig. 28).

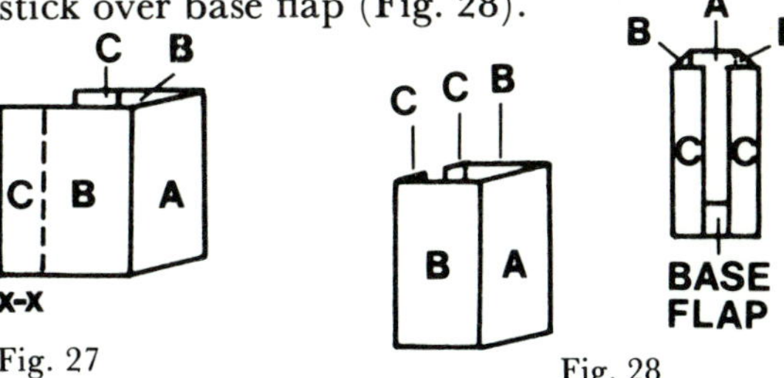

Fig. 27

Fig. 28

4. Cut side section from the discarded top of the box, and stick over C–C, to form fourth side of tower.

5. Cut battlements to match the walls (Fig. 29).

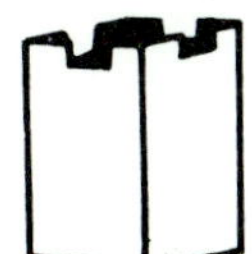

Fig. 29

6. Cover with lining paper, as before.

7. Paint walls and towers thickly with light grey poster colour.

Archway

Cut out in mid-grey paper – about $2\frac{1}{2} \times 2\frac{1}{4}$in (6.5 × 5.5cm) width × height. Cut the entrance a little smaller round sides and top, in dark grey, and rule lines for the portcullis. Stick entrance to archway, lower edges level, and mark bricks all round.

Drawbridge

Cut out in thick card – about $2\frac{1}{2} \times 3$in (6.5 × 8cm) width × length. Cover with brown paper.

'Hinge' to lower edge of entrance with tape underneath. Punch holes in each side of drawbridge, about 1in (25mm) from the end, and two more about 1in (25mm) above base of arch, one on each side. Thread string through archway holes and stick ends to back: then stick archway to centre front of one wall. Thread loose ends of string through drawbridge holes and tie underneath.

Windows

Cut out in black paper (see pattern): stick to walls and towers as illustrated.

Indicate stonework with grey oil pastel (or darker poster colour).

Flags

Cut out in coloured paper – about $3\frac{1}{2} \times 1$in (9 × 2.5cm). Stick graduated beads on a pin: push Plasticine inside the top of a drinking straw to hold pin, and stick to secure. Roll a strip of Plasticine round the straw to make a firm base (Fig. 30). Stand flags inside towers.

Stand birthday cake on up-turned baking tin, and assemble fort around it, as shown.

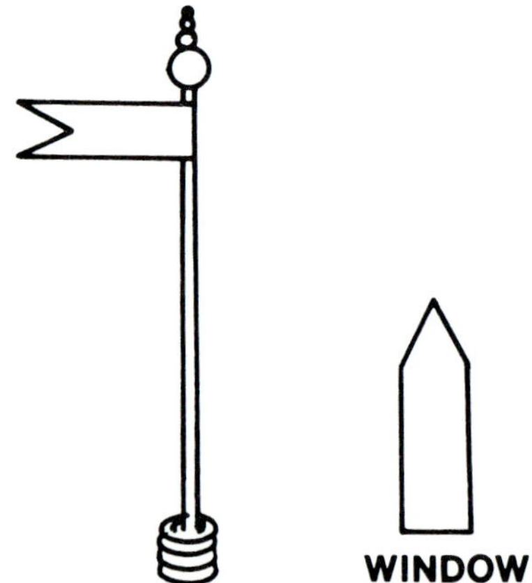

Fig. 30

32

REGIMENTAL BAND

These smartly uniformed soldiers need not be musical. Without their instruments, they could stand to attention in a circle around the cake. They make excellent place card holders, too: fix narrow strips of card displaying the names of your guests between their outstretched hands.

Materials

White cartridge or construction paper
Lightweight paper in red, blue, brown and
    black – for uniform, hair and cap
Shiny black paper for cap peak and shoes
Stiff black paper for crown of cap
Coloured papers to cover drums
Gold foil paper
White face tissue for feather cockade
White tissue paper for drums
Small round coloured adhesive labels
    (optional)
Toilet roll inner tube (optional)
2 small 2-pronged paper fasteners (for each
    soldier)
2 cocktail sticks for baton and drumsticks
2 wooden toothpicks for drumsticks
Large and small beads for baton and
    drumsticks
Plastic-covered or galvanised wire for
    triangle
Gold and silver cord gift-tie for chinstrap and
    drums
Flesh-coloured poster paint
Pins
Plasticine (optional)
Transparent adhesive tape
Wallpaper paste
Copydex adhesive
Evo-stik clear adhesive

1. Cut a piece of white paper 5 × 8in (13 × 20cm) depth × width: rule horizontal lines as Fig. 31.
2. Paint flesh-colour between *b–c* as indicated – overlapping above and below.

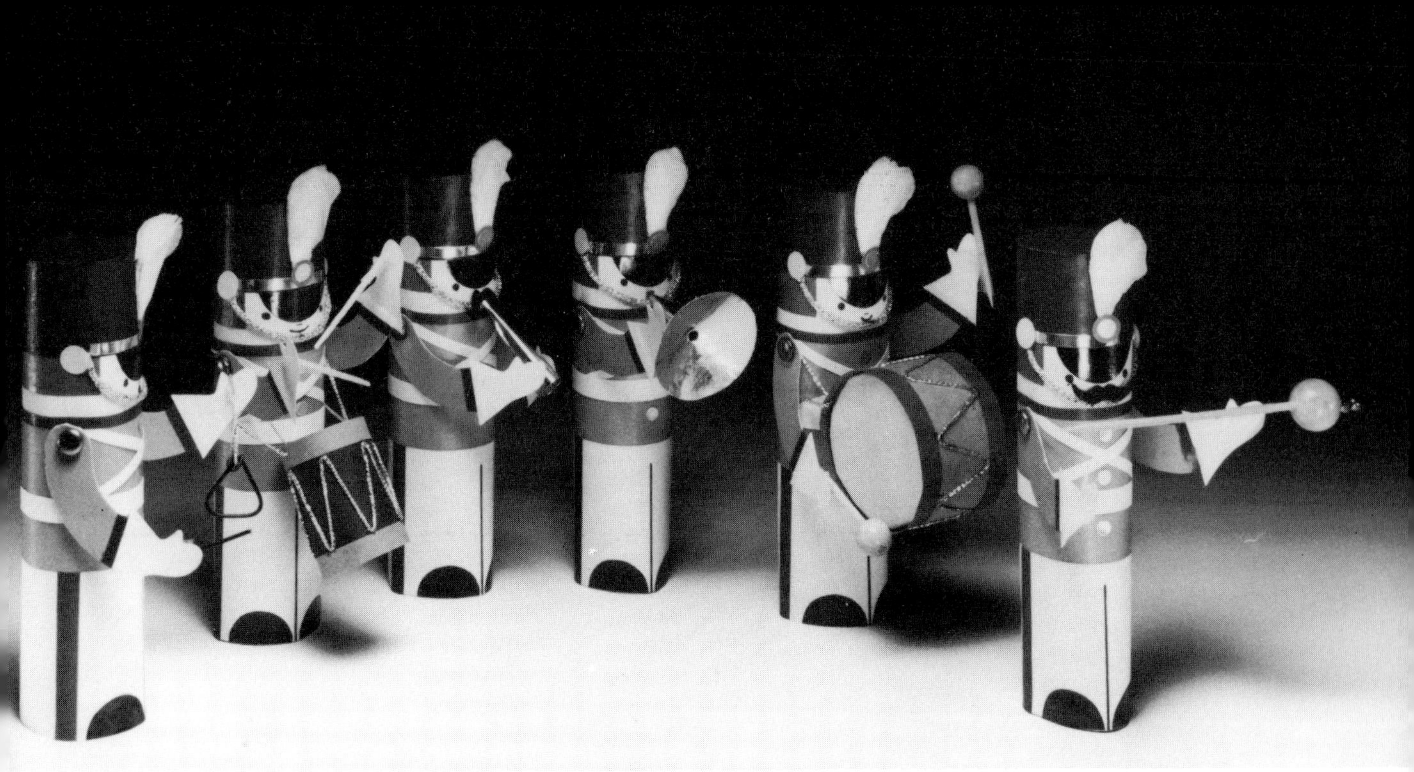

Regimental band

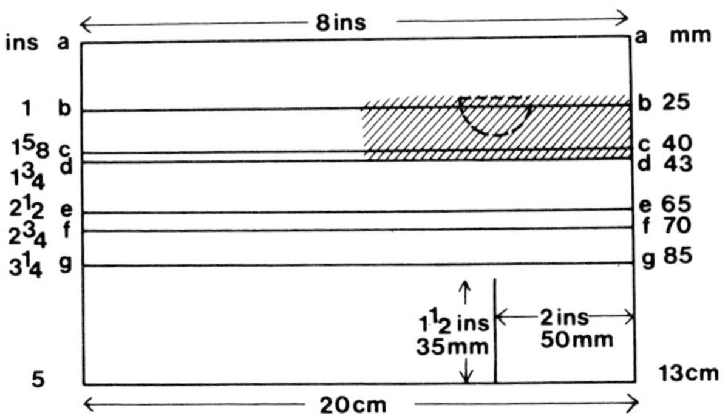

Fig. 31

3. Rule vertical black line for leg division, as indicated.

4. Cut a 1in (25mm) diameter semi-circle of shiny black paper for peak of cap: stick over painted area as indicated.

5. Cut a $\frac{3}{4}$in (20mm) diameter circle in half for his boots. Stick each side of leg division, curved side uppermost.

6. Roll up and make into a $1\frac{1}{4}$in (3cm) diameter cylinder (basic method 6 – p. 67).

7. Cut brown paper $2\frac{5}{8} \times \frac{1}{2}$in (6.5 × 1.5cm) width × depth. Paste round back of head for hair, top edge overlapping b–b.

8. Cut red paper $4 \times 1\frac{5}{8}$in (10 × 4cm) width × depth: paste between c–g, join at back. Stick two $\frac{1}{8}$in (3mm) wide strips of white paper diagonally across chest, as shown (between pp. 20–21), ending at each side between c–d and e–f. Then stick white belt strip round e–f and blue colour round c–d. Punch tiny gold buttons for jacket, and stick $\frac{1}{4}$in (5mm) blue stripes down sides of trousers.

9. To make each arm, paste red paper to white: draw two semi-circles as Fig. 32. Cut out as shown, fold in half, and stick together.

Fig. 32

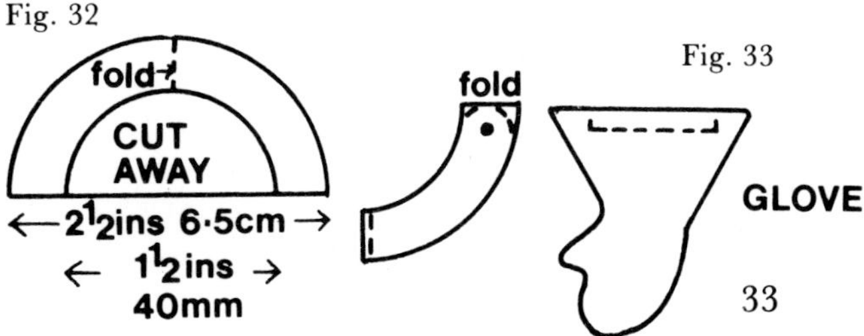

33

Round off top as shown, and punch a small hole. Cut the glove twice in white, stick the *hand only* together – then slip arm inside gauntlet (to broken line) and stick. Stick blue strip (as collar) round arm.

10. Position an arm at each side, and mark hole on body. Make a small slit there, and fix arms with 2-pronged paper fasteners.

11. Cut black paper 4 × 1in (10 × 2.5cm) width × depth: paste between *a–b*, for hat. Cut a 1¼in (3cm) diameter circle of stiff black paper for the crown, and stick to top edge. Stick gold strip across front. Fold white face tissue into four – then in half again: place cockade pattern against last fold, and cut out. Fold lengthways, as broken line, open out slightly, and stick to front. Stick gold gift-tie round face for chinstrap, and decorate as illustrated.

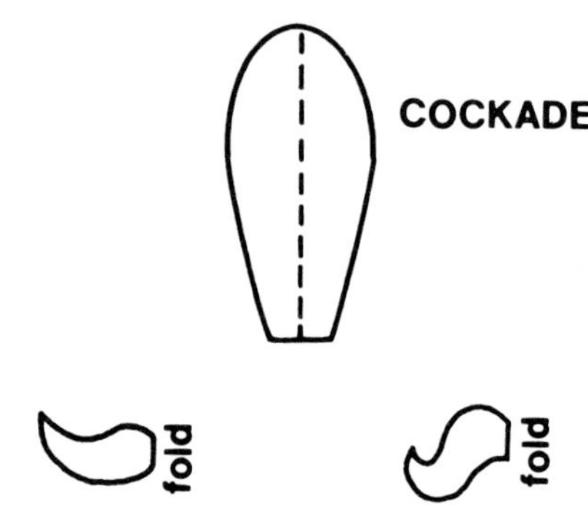

Fig. 34

12. Draw features (basic method 13 – p. 70), following the photograph.
13. Cut moustaches in folded black paper: stick centre to face (*after* fixing wind instruments).
14. Make the instruments, as follows:

Trumpet: Cut two 1¼in (3cm) diameter circles in gold, and stick back-to-back. Cut from outer edge to centre – and then cut a tiny circle (Fig. 35): curve round and stick overlap, as broken line. Cut a 1¼in (3cm) radius quarter-circle in half, and trim off corner as shown. Curve round and stick overlap: stick over hole in first piece.

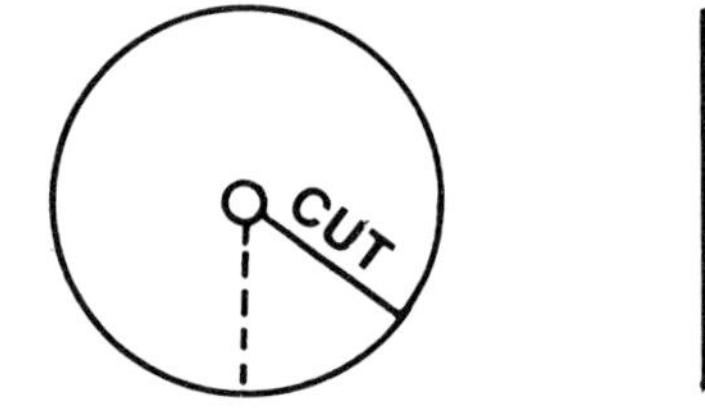

Fig. 35

Horn: Cut a 1½in (4cm) radius quarter-circle in half, and stick back-to-back. Cut off corner (as trumpet), then curve round and stick overlap.

Big drum: Cut 1in (25mm) off a toilet roll tube. For *each* side, cut *two* 1¼in (35mm) circles of white tissue paper and stick the edges lightly together. Spread adhesive round edge: stand tube in centre, and bring tissue up evenly all round. Cover outside with coloured paper, adding a narrow contrasting strip overlapping each edge. Decorate with gift-tie as illustrated. Cut a cocktail stick in half for drumsticks, and fix a large bead on each.

Small drum: Cut paper 1¼ × 8in (3 × 20cm) depth × length, and make into a 1in (25mm) diameter cylinder. Then make up drum as above. Cut toothpicks to length for drumsticks.

Triangle: Bend wire into triangle, and loop round the hand with cord, as illustrated. Cut a short piece of wire for the striker.

Bandleader's baton: Stick two or three graduated beads at one end of a cocktail stick.
15. Hang drums round the neck, taking cord over arms, through sides of drum, and under arms to tie at back. Fix baton, drumsticks and other instruments to hands with clear adhesive tape. For wind instruments, push a small pin into the mouth, leaving half protruding: slip mouthpiece over and stick.
16. If the instruments make the figures fall forward, restore balance with a lump of Plasticine pinned inside back at base of tube.

DESIGN YOUR OWN TOTEM POLE

Think up your own weird and wonderful designs and draw them on separate strips of paper, using bright, contrasting colours. Find a suitable card tube – or make your own (basic method 6 – p. 67). The totem pole shown (between pp. 20–21) is the inner from a roll of paper kitchen towels. The three heads are on white paper, but different colours are used for the strips between and for the 'wings', mounting one colour over another.

Materials

White or coloured cartridge or construction
    paper
Card tube – as above – about 10in (25cm)
    long by 1⅝in (40mm) in diameter
Coloured drawing inks, markers, poster
    paints, etc.
Black fibre-tip pen
Copydex adhesive

1. Measure very carefully round the outside of your tube – then add about ½in (10mm) for the overlap.
2. To make a head, cut a strip of paper the above width – and about 1½–2in (4–5cm) deep. Fold in half and lightly sketch an eye fairly close to the fold (Fig. 36). Now draw a pattern round the eye, extending your design over the rest of the paper.

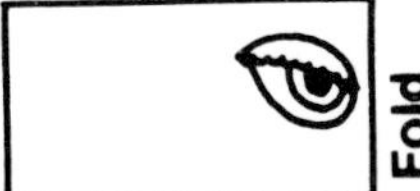

Fig. 36

3. Using a soft lead pencil, trace your design, mark the edges and fold. Turn the paper, and your tracing over, place the tracing right side down on the paper, edges matching, and transfer the design (basic method 1 – p. 66).
4. Open out and colour. Then go over all the lines in black.

5. Place the folded head strip on another piece of paper, and draw the beak against the fold: remove the head, and add about ½in (10mm) at the back (Fig. 37). Cut twice and stick *the beak only* together – folding back the excess along the broken line. Colour and decorate beak. Cut a slit in centre fold of head strip, slot beak through, and stick tabs to back of strip.

BEAK

Fig. 37

WING

6. Make the 'wings' in double paper Fig. 37, adding tabs as for beak. Cut a strip to go round the pole: then cut in two – leaving *all* the overlap allowance on one piece. Stick the shorter piece between the wings for the body front, then halve the longer strip, and stick one side to each back wing tab.
7. Make other strips of varying depths to fit between – incorporating 'feet' in the design for the lowest strip, and cutting a narrow, shaped strip for the top. Study the photograph for guidance and ideas if you need them.
8. Wrap the strips smoothly round the tube, sticking the overlap at the back to hold in place.

REDSKIN MICE

The basic mouse (p. 14) is made in reddish-brown paper, and both chief and brave wear feather headdresses painted on medium-weight white paper. The birthday message is written on coloured paper stuck round toothpicks – the broad end fixed through the body front. If banners unbalance mice, fix a small lump of Plasticine round the knotted tail, inside the body.

MISS MANY HAPPY RETURNS

These decorations are illustrated in colour plate 4 facing page 21

Birthday party decorations with a feminine theme. First, the fort of the last chapter, transformed into a glistening silver and white palace of ice.

THE SNOW QUEEN'S CASTLE

An ice palace among shining silver rocks makes a glamorous setting for a little girl's birthday cake. The towers are the inner tubes from rolls of paper kitchen towels, although you can make these yourself if you wish. Again, the sizes of the decoration illustrated are given as a guide.

Materials

4 cardboard cartons for walls about
$8\frac{1}{2} \times 4\frac{3}{4} \times 1\frac{1}{4}$in ($21 \times 12 \times 3$cm) width × height × depth
4 card tubes (see above) for towers – about 7in (18cm) long by $1\frac{3}{4}$in (45mm) in diameter (see above)
Cartridge or construction or similar weight paper
Wall or shelf lining paper
Kitchen foil
Gold foil paper for doors
Blue foil paper for windows
White poster paint
Wallpaper paste
Copydex adhesive

Walls

1. Open out flaps and cut box as Fig. 38.

2. Score back and front about $1\frac{1}{2}$in (4cm) below top – then cut side flaps down to scored line. Bend the scored sections back until they meet: stick narrow top strips under front and over back. Fold flaps back into position, and stick. Cut ends level with sloping roof – as broken lines, Fig. 39.

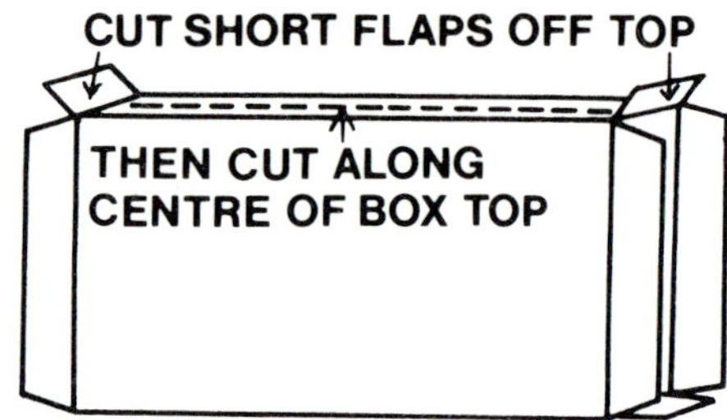

Fig. 38

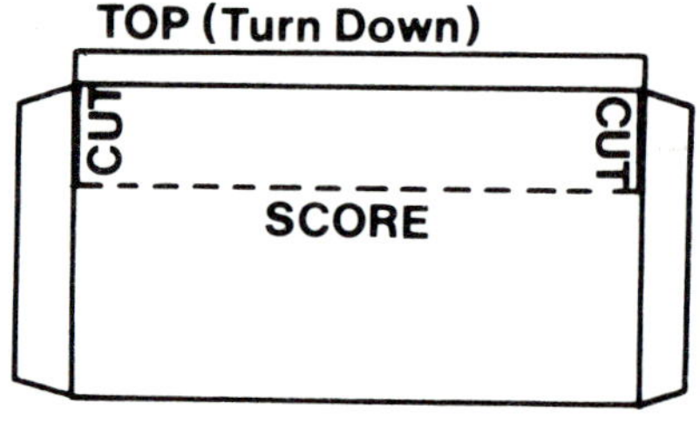

Fig. 39

3. Paste lining paper over the box, folding it neatly round edges and corners.

Towers

1. Cut four 7in (18cm) high towers from card inner tubes – or make 1¾in (4.5cm) diameter cylinders as basic method 6 – p. 67.
2. Paste lining paper round towers – overlapping the top edge about ⅜in (10mm): snip this surplus into small tabs (Fig. 40).

Paint walls and towers thickly with white poster colour, *dabbing* your brush over the wet surface, to resemble ice.

Tower roofs

Cut a 6in (15cm) semi-circle of cartridge paper for each tower roof. Stick a slightly larger semi-circle of foil to the paper. Cut centre as arrow (Fig. 40). Mark overlap, then curve round into a cone and stick: turn surplus foil up inside. Spread adhesive on tabs of tower, and press cone down over them.

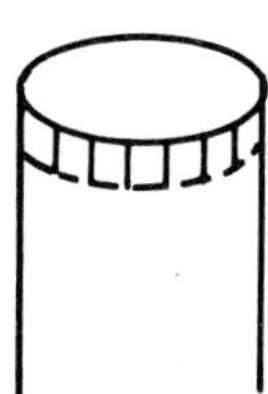

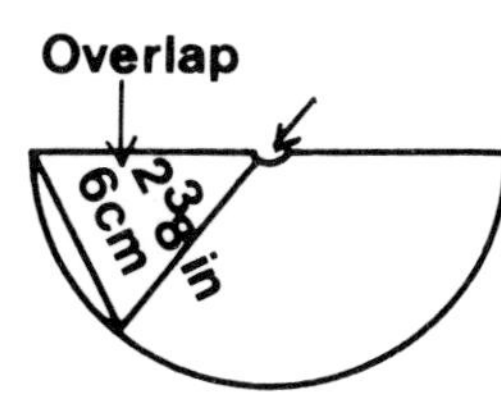

Fig. 40

Main roofs

For each main roof, cut a piece of *double* foil about 4½in (11cm) deep by the width of the box. Fold like a concertina to cut 'icicle' edge on each long side, as illustrated (facing p. 21): smooth out creases, fold lengthways and stick over box.

Doors

Cut doors about 2¾ × 1¾in (7 × 4.5cm) – depth × width, in gold paper, following the illustration, and stick to one wall.

Windows

Cut windows for walls in blue foil, about 1½ × ⅝in (35 × 15mm) – depth × width. Cut three windows for each tower, about 1 × ½in (25 × 12mm) – depth × width.

Crumple strips of foil, about 12 × 4½in (30 × 12cm) – length × width, to form rocks surrounding towers.

Stand birthday cake on up-turned baking tin, and assemble castle around it, as illustrated.

SNOW MAIDENS MOBILE

A delicate mobile of starry snowflakes strung between snow maidens in softly coloured dresses.

Materials

Thin white card
Coloured face tissues for dresses (or crayons
   or waterproof drawing inks)
Brown paper napkin for hair (optional)
White paper doilies
Kitchen foil
Fancy silver embossed foil for wings (optional)
Silver stars
Flesh-coloured poster paint
Fine black sewing thread
Thin garden stake – at least 18in (45cm) long
Wallpaper paste
Copydex adhesive

Snow maidens

1. Trace and transfer figure 41 on to thin card (basic method 1 – p. 66). Cut out carefully.

Snow maidens

Fig. 41

38

2. Paint the face and hands. Turn over and paint the hands and *neck only* on the back.

3. Paste dress liberally and press face tissue smoothly on to it – overlapping all round. Turn over and repeat on back. When dry, trim level with card.

4. Cut motifs from doilies: paste *dress* – press motifs down and trim overlap.

5. Use narrow strips of brown napkin for the hair, as basic method 12 – p. 69, or colour with paint or crayon.

6. Crumple bits of foil into tiny balls and stick to hair, as shown.

7. Mark eyes in black.

8. Cut a pair of wings for each figure in folded fancy, or kitchen, foil. Stick fold to centre back of figure.

9. When you have made as many figures as you want, knot sewing thread through tops of heads (dot on pattern), and tie at intervals along the garden stake to hang at different levels. Tie a length of thread between the ends of the stake, to hang.

Stars

Stick silver stars back-to-back at intervals along short lengths of thread and fix each end to the hand of a snowmaiden, linking the figures as illustrated.

EMILY-KATE

Find a pretty patterned paper for the dress – then colour sleeves and hat to match. Stand this charming little birthday girl in the centre of the tea-table or on top of the cake.

Materials

Cartridge or construction paper for body
Patterned (gift-wrap) paper for dress
Flesh pink face tissue for arms
Coloured face tissues or napkins for sleeves,
  basket, flowers and leaves
Brown paper napkin for hair
Cartridge or construction paper for hat
Coloured paper for hat ribbon
White paper doilies
Table tennis ball for head
2 pipe-cleaners for arms
Matchstick
Tiny pins (optional)
Flesh-coloured poster paint
Wallpaper paste
Copydex adhesive

1. Draw the body as Fig. 42, the centre semi-circle ½in (15mm) in diameter: measure and mark overlap. Cut out.

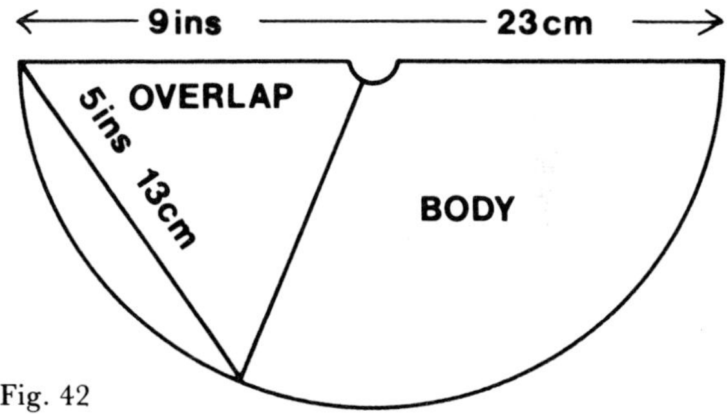

Fig. 42

2. Ignoring the overlap, paste patterned paper over rest of semi-circle: trim level with edge. Curve round into a cone and stick overlap.

3. When dry, make armholes, ¾in (20mm) below the top edge.

4. Using *two* 5in (13cm) lengths of pipe-cleaner side by side, make arms (basic method 11 – p. 69).

5. Cut tissue for sleeves 5 × 1¼in (13 × 3cm) – width × depth. Overlap the long edges, and stick to form a tube. Slip the arms through, then bind the end of each sleeve tightly round the wrist with thread, as illustrated. Push the arms through the body.

6. Cut a 5½–6in (14–15cm) diameter semi-circle of doily for pinafore: then cut off a ½in (10mm) wide strip along the straight edge. Fit round body as illustrated, sticking top edge

and overlapping corners at the back. Add narrow straps over shoulders and a scrap for her collar.

7. Fix head on matchstick and paint. When dry, push matchstick down into body, *in front* of the arms.

8. Make hair, with ringlets at each side, as basic method 12 – p. 69, following the illustration for guidance.

9. Cut a 3½in (9cm) circle of paper for her hat, with a 1¼in (3cm) hole in the centre. Fit on head, sticking sides down as shown. Stick a paper 'ribbon' round under the chin.

10. Using same method as for hair, wind pasted strips of tissue round and round, moulding with the fingertips to form a curved oval shape for her basket. Twist a double strip for the handle, sticking ends at each side. When dry, line with green tissue and fill with face tissue flowers (basic method 15 – p. 71).

11. Mark the eyes in black and mouth in brown (basic method 13 – p. 70).

SNOWFLAKE FAIRY MOUSE

The basic mouse (p. 14) is made in dark brown. Silver doily wings and star-tipped wand are made like those of Fairy Silver-Wings (p. 26).

Emily-Kate

TRADITIONAL FEAST AND FESTIVAL

These decorations are illustrated in colour plate 5 facing page 44

Various dates on the calendar have a special significance reaching far back into the past, making them traditional occasions for some kind of festivity. In country districts there is the Harvest Festival, in the United States, Thanksgiving, and All Saints' Day is preceded, on October 31st, by Hallowe'en. Here are some decorations to help set the right mood for these occasions, especially for Hallowe'en when witches and ghosts are on the loose and an eerie atmosphere is needed.

WITCH'S MOON LAMPSHADE

A dramatic lampshade that can stay in use long after Hallowe'en. It is both amusing and practical all the year round – just right for the nursery or playroom.

Materials

Two 9in (23cm) diameter lampshade rings,
   one with pendant fitting
Thin white card about 30 × 8in (75 × 20cm)
Deep blue paper – size as above
Black paper
Bright yellow or white paper
Black felt or fibre-tip pen or marker or
   drawing ink
Strong sewing thread
Wallpaper paste
Copydex adhesive

1. Cut both the white card and blue paper to size: this should be the circumference of your lampshade ring *plus* ¾in (2cm) – by the depth you require; the shade shown (*facing p. 44*) is 8in (20cm) deep.

Fig. 43

42

2. Very carefully, cut out a 2¾in (7cm) diameter circle in the blue paper, just above the centre (see Fig. 43), to make the moon.
3. Paste the blue paper smoothly to the card: leave to dry.
4. Sketch the outlines of tree trunks and branches, following the illustration and diagram for guidance. When you are satisfied, mark them boldly in black, adding foliage, ferns, grass, an owl, or anything eerie.
5. Trace witch on to black paper (basic method 1– p. 66). Cut out and stick over moon. Add tiny yellow or white circles for owl's eyes.
6. Oversew long edges round the two rings (pendant at the top): stick the overlap neatly.
7. Cut strips of black paper about ½in (10–15mm) wide with pinking shears, and stick round, overlapping top and bottom edges.

MAGIC AND MISCHIEF – HALLOWE'EN MOBILE

Evil witches, miserable as sin, and grinning cats make a mobile to droop over a dark doorway and send shudders up the spine.

Materials

Black, grey and white cartridge or
   construction paper
Stiff black paper (or double thickness of
   above)
White face tissue
Coloured inks, markers, paints or crayons
   (including white)
Fine black sewing thread
Thin garden stake at least 18in (45cm) long
Copydex adhesive

Witches

1. Trace head on to *double* (stuck together) grey paper (basic method 1 – p. 66). Cut out.
2. Trace eyes and noses on to white paper. Paint in lurid colours, and outline heavily in black. Cut out.
3. For witch A, cut face tissue 3½ × 4in (9 × 10cm) depth × width: cut in narrow strips to ¼in (5mm) from top edge (see Fig. 44), then

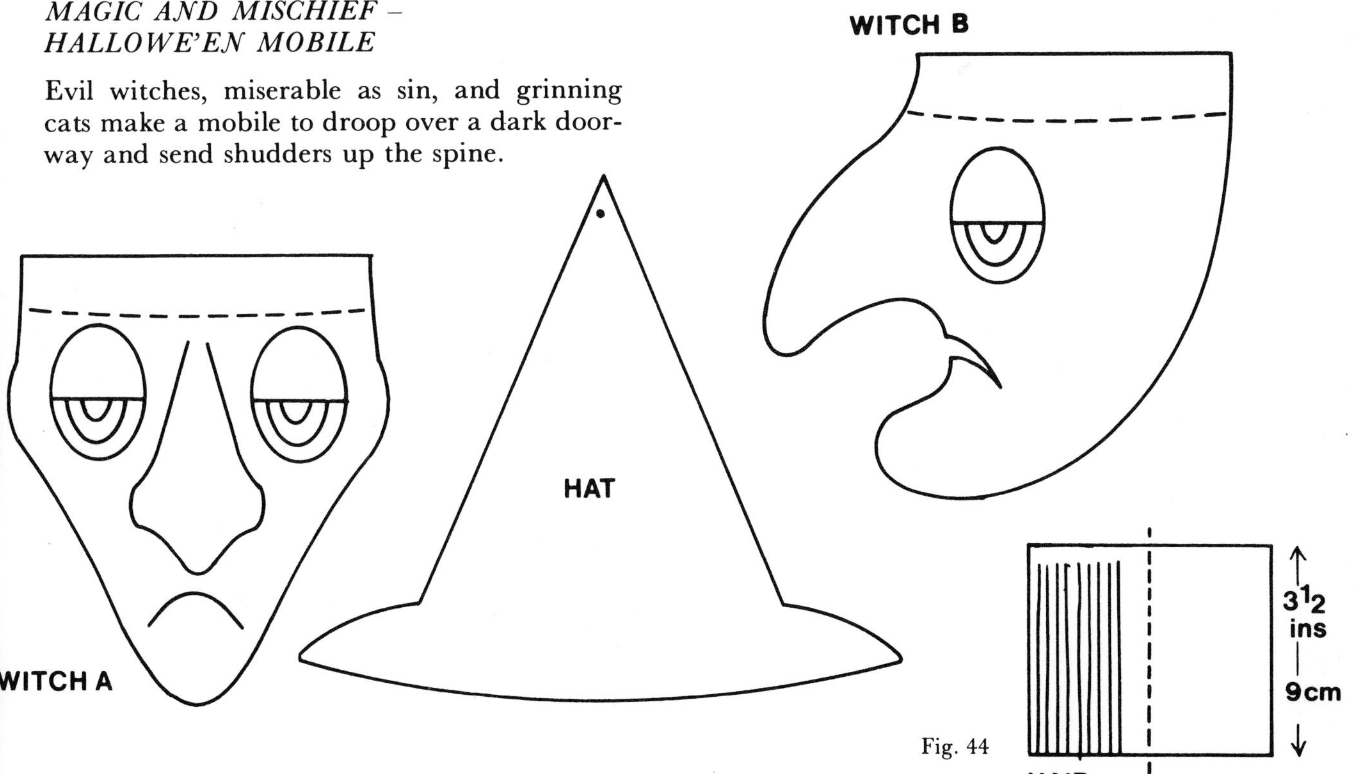

fold in half, as broken line. Stick top edge across back of head.

4. For witch B, prepare a 3½in (9cm) square of tissue as above, but stick to front and back, folding round the edge.

5. Cut hat in *double* black paper: stick together, top of head between brim, as broken line.

6. Stick features into position and draw mouth.

Cats

1. Trace on to stiff black paper and cut out.

2. Trace eyes and nose on to white paper: colour and cut out.

Fig. 45

3. Draw mouth and ears in white. Then stick features into position.

When you have made all your witches and cats, knot thread through tops of hats and heads (as dots on patterns), and tie at intervals along the garden stake, to hang at different levels. Tie a length of thread between the ends of the stake, to hang the mobile.

GHOSTS

These ghosts are so quick and easy to make, you will have a haunted house in next to no time.

Materials

White cartridge or construction paper
Black fibre-tip pen or drawing ink
Copydex adhesive

1. For the largest figure, cut a semi-circle as Fig. 46, cutting away centre as shown. Measure and mark overlap.

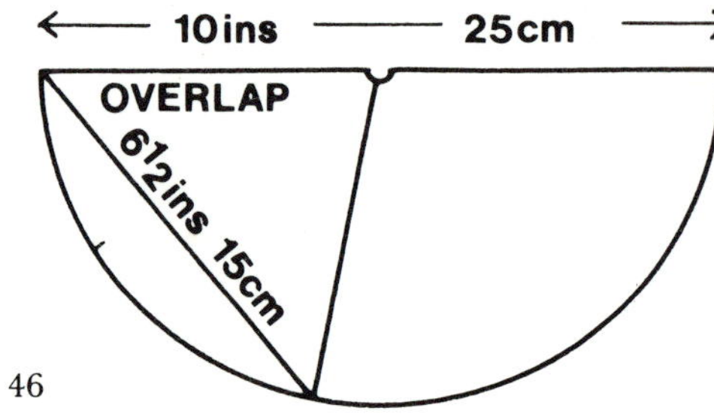

Fig. 46

2. Curve round into a cone, and stick overlap.

3. Cut lower edge into points, as illustrated (facing p. 44).

4. To make arms, draw a 6in (15cm) diameter half-circle: then place the point of your compasses at the centre of the curve – *x* on Fig. 47 – and draw another half-circle.

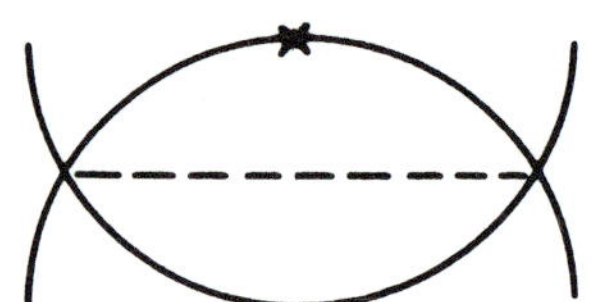

Fig. 47

5. Cut out, score broken line and fold. Now fold again, and sketch shape, as Fig. 48. Cut, then open out *second* fold only.

Fig. 48

Plate 5 opposite: Hallowe'en mobile: Witch's moon lampshade: Hallowe'en mice: Fir tree: Ghosts

44

6. Slit sides of body and slot arms through.
7. Draw the eyes on a separate piece of paper. Cut out and stick into position.

For smaller figures, decrease the diameter of the body semi-circle 1in each time (or 2cm), keeping the overlap in proportion, and reduce the arm measurement by ½in (10mm).

FIR TREE

In the forests of central Europe, cottagers make tiny model trees from curled wood shavings. This paper imitation makes an appropriate decoration for traditional celebrations like Harvest Festival or Thanksgiving. The tree in the picture (facing p. 44) was made from the inside of old manilla envelopes, but parcel wrapping paper, or even brown paper bags, would do as well.

Materials

Buff-coloured paper for tree (see above)
Brown paper napkin for trunk (or white face tissue and brown paint or ink)
Coloured paper for base
Cotton reel
Pencil – about 5in (13cm) long
Wallpaper paste
Copydex adhesive

1. Draw master pattern *on tracing paper*, as Fig. 49. On a 9in (23cm) diameter semi-circle, rule twelve lines radiating from the centre – measuring them with a protractor every 10 degrees, up to 120 degrees. Then draw curved lines B–J at ⅜in (10mm) intervals.

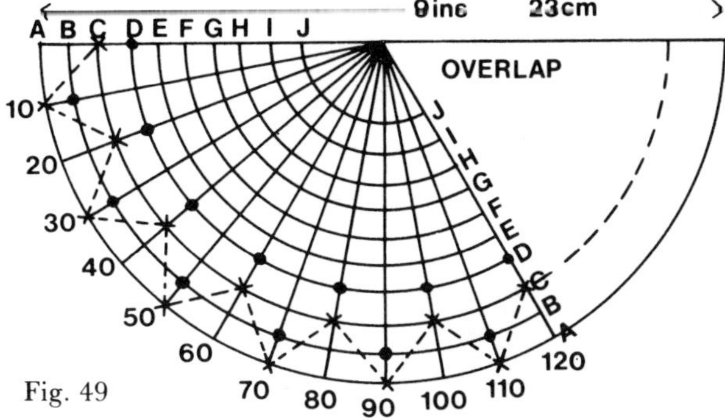

Fig. 49

2. Draw a 9in (23cm) semi-circle on buff paper. Place master pattern on top, hold firmly in place, and prick lines A and C alternately at each point marked *x* – exactly where the straight and curved lines meet. Remove pattern: draw a line between centre and point C, to mark overlap – then continue line C around overlap, as indicated.
3. Cut out, cutting between the pin-pricks, and round the overlap, as broken lines. Cut a tiny semi-circle at the centre. Your cut-out paper should now look like Fig. 50.
4. Curve round, and stick the overlap (very accurately). Curl the points up as illustrated (facing p. 44), using basic method 5 – p. 67.
5. Make another, identical, cone. Brush adhesive round top of first one, then slide second down over it, the curled points exactly *between* those of the one below.
6. For the next layer, draw a semi-circle 8¼in (21cm) in diameter. Using your pattern, prick lines B and D at points *o*: mark the overlap as before, and continue line D around it. Cut out as Fig. 50, make up cone and stick over first two

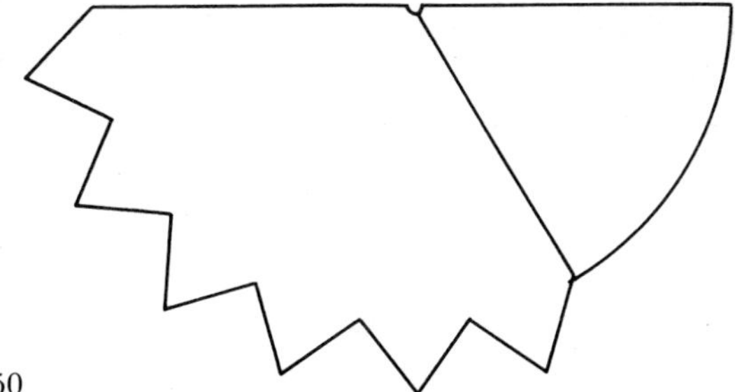
Fig. 50

D

– the points exactly between those of the last one (matching the bottom layer).

7. Draw your next semi-circle 7½in (19cm) in diameter. Prick lines c and e, mark overlap, then make up and position cone as before.

8. Continue to cut decreasing semi-circles, ending with one 3¾in (9cm) in diameter, cutting the points between h and j.

9. Fix pencil in cotton reel – point up. Bind with brown napkin (basic method 4 – p. 66): brush liberally with paste, and crumple pasted napkin over top of reel.

10. When dry, stick coloured paper round reel, as illustrated.

11. Cover bound tip of pencil with adhesive, and press foliage firmly down over it.

HALLOWE'EN MICE

A pipe-cleaner pushed through the body of the ghostly white mouse (facing p. 44) is draped with trailing white face tissue. The black witch mouse carries a broom made from grass seed-heads tied round the end of a matchstick.

GOOD LUCK AND BEST WISHES

Engagements, weddings, anniversaries, are all good excuses for a celebration and for romantic decorations to mark the occasion.

WEDDING BELLS BRIDE

A demure Victorian bride in lace and roses is easily concocted from paper doilies and face tissues.

Materials

White and pink cartridge or construction
  paper
White, rose pink, flesh pink and green face
  tissues
Brown paper napkin for hair
White paper doilies
Scrap of thin card
Table tennis ball for head
2 pipe-cleaners for arms
Thin garden stake 7in (18cm) long
Flesh-coloured poster paint
Adhesive tape
Wallpaper paste
Copydex adhesive

1. For the underskirt, cut a 10in (25cm) diameter semi-circle in white paper as Fig. 51, cutting away a 1in (25mm) semi-circle at the centre; mark a 7in (17cm) overlap. Curve round into a cone, and stick.
2. Cut a 3in (8cm) diameter circle of paper for the flounce pattern. Place a *single* ply of pink and white tissue together: pin pattern on top and cut round it with pinking shears (fold the tissue to cut several sets of circles at once). Fold circle in half, pink inside, then gather so the centre forms a point as shown (Fig. 51). Stick several of these closely all round bottom edge of underskirt (sticking points only).
3. Cut a section of doily to form a slightly wider overskirt, covering top of flounces, as illustrated. Back with pink paper, and make into a cone to sit neatly over the lower one: stick at top.
4. Cut a 3½in (9cm) diameter semi-circle for the bodice, cutting away a ½in (15mm) semi-circle at the centre, and marking a 1¾in (45mm) overlap (as Fig. 51). Make up cone – then *flatten* (Fig. 52), and cut half-way down the fold at each side, to *x*'s, as indicated.

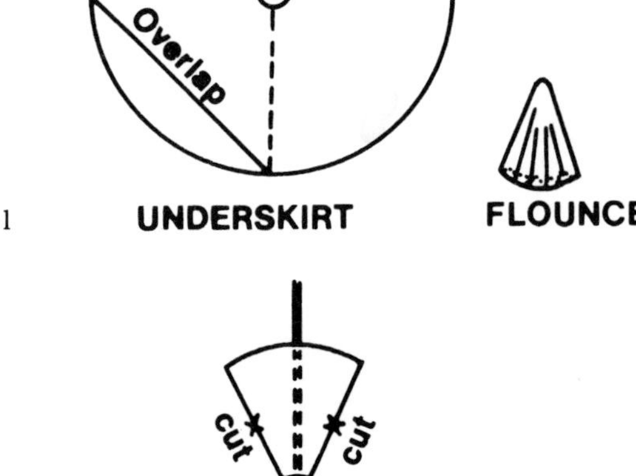

Fig. 51   **UNDERSKIRT**   **FLOUNCE**

Fig. 52

5. Using *two* full-length pipe-cleaners side-by-side, make arms (basic method 11 – p. 69). Cut white tissue 7 × 3in (18 × 8cm) and make sleeves

"

Wedding bells bride

as Emily-Kate (p. 39 – instruction 5). Push arms into position through slits in bodice.

6. Push garden stake through cone as Fig. 52. Then tape top edges together for shoulders. Decorate front and back with scraps of doily.

7. Lower stake into skirt, and tape at front. Stick folded pink tissue round waist to form a sash and join the cones securely.

8. Paint head and fit on stake. Wrap flesh tissue round neck, adding a scrap of doily for collar. Make hair as basic method 12 – p. 69, with a bun on top, as illustrated.

9. Cut a lacy section of doily for veil (see illustration for guidance): stick top edge to hair.

Make pink roses from 1in (25mm) squares of tissue (basic method 18 – p. 71), and slightly smaller green rosettes (basic method 16 – p. 71); mount on doily to form headdress, as shown.

10. Draw train on white paper as Fig. 53. Cut with pinking shears. Border with flounced circles as skirt – slightly overlapping edge: begin round base with 2in (5cm) diameter circles, gradually decreasing up the sides to $1\frac{1}{4}$in (3cm) at the top. Add one or two more layers round base. Cover centre with sections of doily backed by pink paper. Stick top to figure, finishing with a folded tissue bow and roses (basic method 18 – p. 71), as shown.

48

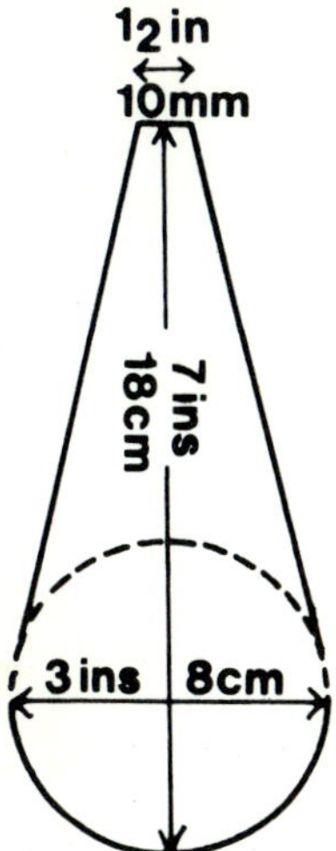

11. Make seven roses for her bouquet from 1½in (4cm) squares of tissue. Cover a 1¼in (3cm) diameter circle of card with a 4in (10cm) circle of green tissue, binding excess tightly underneath with thread. Edge with doily, and cover top with ruched green (basic method 17 – p. 71), pressing roses into the wet tissue. When dry, fix to hand.

12. Mark the eyes in black (basic method 13 – p. 70).

LOVEBIRDS AND DAISIES ANNIVERSARY HEART

A pair of lovebirds for Saint Valentine's Day, an engagement party or a wedding anniversary.

Materials

Deep pink cartridge or construction paper
White paper for daisies
White, blue, yellow and green face tissues
Stiff card (see below)
2 tiny black beads
Wallpaper paste
Copydex adhesive

1. Fold tracing paper – at least 4½in (12cm) square – in half: rule ¾in (2cm) squares and draw up half heart following Fig. 54. Turn paper over, trace through to other side, then transfer full heart to stiff card (basic method 1 – p. 66). If you find cutting thick card difficult, cut twice in thinner and stick together. Cut out.

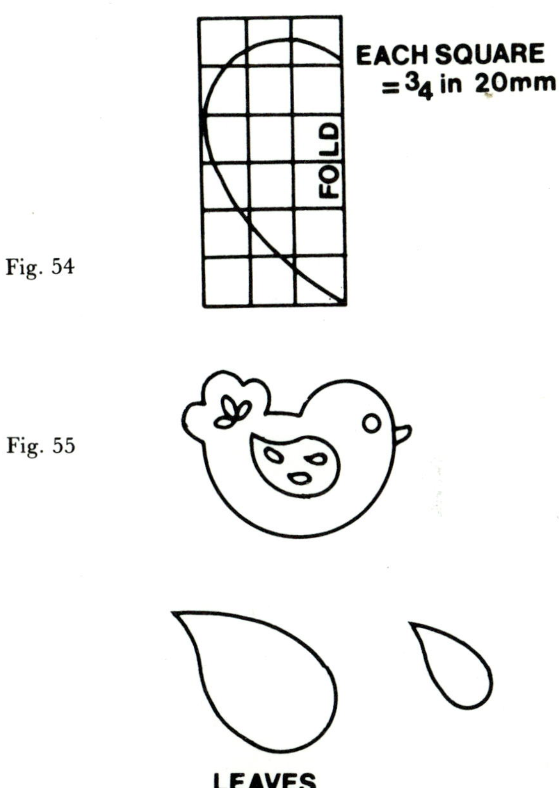

Fig. 54

Fig. 55

2. Paste pink paper smoothly over card: trim edge level.

3. Trace lovebird and transfer to heart as illustrated (facing p. 45) – once in reverse. Push tiny scraps of ruched blue tissue (basic method 17 – p. 71) closely together to fill in the wings. Press in minute scraps of white for feathers. Fill in the body with ruched white tissue, following the outline carefully. Add blue in tail feathers. Press beads into the wet tissue for eyes. Use minute scraps of yellow for beaks. Leave to dry.

4. Make about thirteen small daisies (basic method 20 – p. 72), adding rosette centres made

49

from ¾in (2cm) squares of yellow tissue (basic method 16 – p. 71).

5. Cut seven large leaves (Fig. 55) in strengthened green face tissue (basic method 7 – p. 67): reverse pattern and cut seven more. Cut five small leaves.

6. Stick a daisy to the base of each large leaf, and arrange round heart, adding the last leaf to the lowest daisy, as illustrated. Stick daisies into position, and the smaller leaves in the centre, as shown (stick leaf base only).

7. Fold a 1½in (4cm) square of card in half and stick to the back to form a small strut or fix cord to hang, if preferred.

SILVER WEDDING MEMENTO

To mark twenty-five happy years, a cluster of white flowers with gleaming centres in a Victorian 'silver filigree' frame.

Materials

White cartridge or construction paper
Silver paper doily
Silver kitchen foil (optional)
Green face tissue
Thick card
Tiny pearl beads
Fine sewing thread
Wallpaper paste
Copydex adhesive

1. Choose a suitable doily and cut out the section you plan to use. Cut card to back it, so that edge of doily overlaps slightly (size shown is 4 × 5in (10 × 13cm) – width × depth).

2. Cover card with white paper (or foil) (basic method 3 – p. 66): then stick doily on top.

3. Make white paper flowers as basic method 19 – p. 71 (four large and three small of version B shown here). Crumple scraps of foil – about 1in (25mm) square – into balls (or use beads) for centres, surrounding with pearls threaded on sewing cotton.

50

4. Cut a circle of paper to display flowers – 3in (7.5cm) diameter in this case. Cover thickly with ruched green tissue (basic method 17 – p. 71), and press flowers into place while still wet.

5. Make a strut from thick card, and stick to back of frame so that it stands steadily (see Fig. 56).

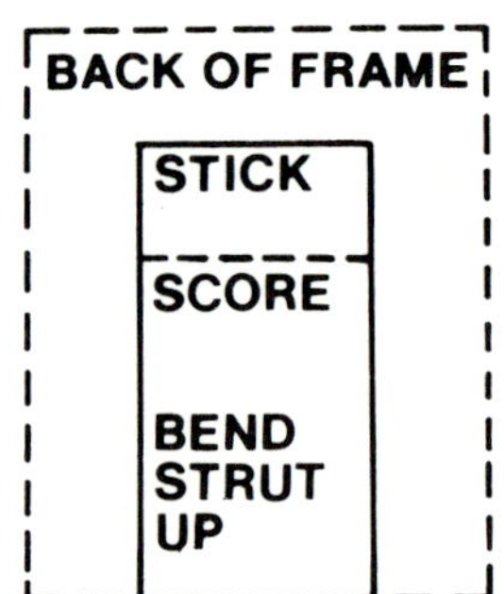

Fig. 56

6. When dry, stick flower arrangement into position.

GOLDEN WEDDING HORSESHOE

Flowers and leaves in subtle shades of buff or cream and light olive, mounted on gold, create a sophisticated effect. In fact these elegant flowers are cut from the inside of old manilla envelopes.

Materials

Gold foil paper
Buff or cream paper (see above)
Green face tissue
Stiff card (see below)
Tiny golden-yellow glass beads
Pearl beads (optional)
Fine wire
Transparent adhesive tape
Wallpaper paste
Evo-stik clear adhesive (for beads)
Copydex adhesive

1. Fold tracing paper – at least 4½in (12cm) square – in half: rule ¾in (2cm) squares and draw up half horseshoe following Fig. 57. Turn paper over, trace through to other side then transfer full horseshoe to stiff card (basic method 1 – p. 66). If you find cutting thick card difficult, cut twice in thinner and stick together. Cut out.

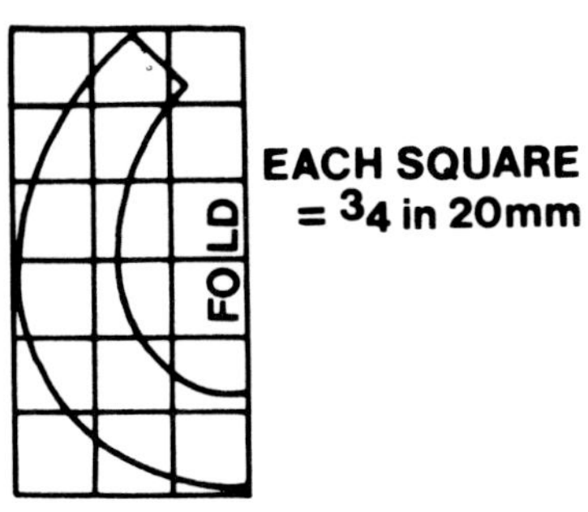

Fig. 57

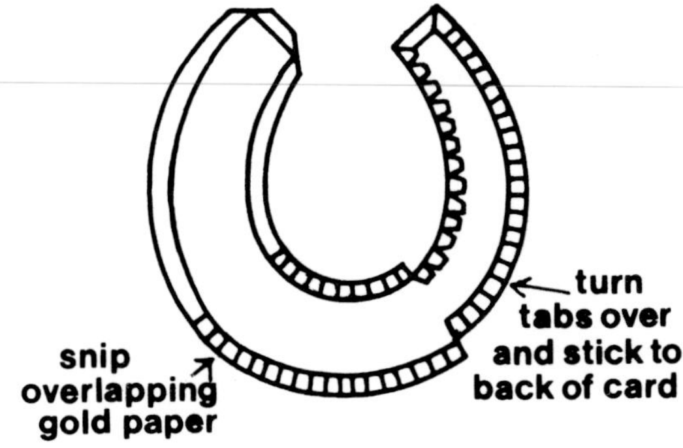

2. Cover with gold paper, leaving about ¼in (5mm) overlapping. Mitre corners (basic method 3 – p. 66): cut rest of surplus into tiny tabs and paste to back.
3. Make *double* cut paper flowers – two each A and B, and one small *single* of each – and three graduated daisies (basic methods 19 and 20 – p. 72). Stick pearls and/or glass beads in centres. Tape a 3½in (9cm) wire stalk to back of each.
4. Bunch flowers and bind stalks together with

tape. Fix a strip of tape across centre of horseshoe as Fig. 58. Arrange flowers at back of horseshoe but in front of tape – as illustrated (facing p. 45), taping the stalks to the back as indicated, and bend protruding wires round neatly.

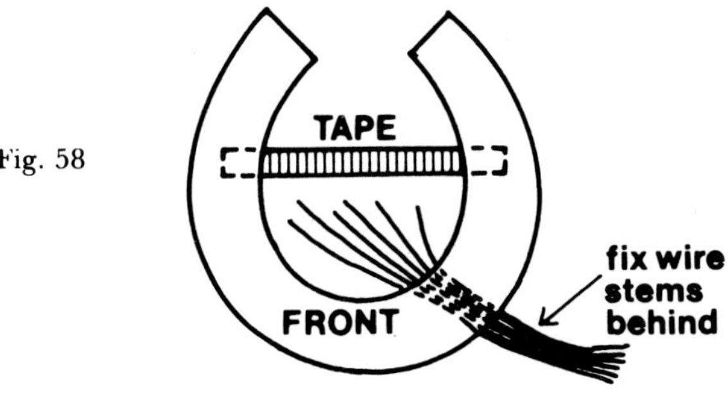

5. Cut leaves in strengthened face tissue (basic method 7 – p. 67), and fit between flowers, sticking behind petals.
6. Make a strut as for Silver Wedding memento – but about 2¾ × ¾in (7 × 1.5cm) – length × width. Tape to centre back, behind previous strip.

BRIDAL MICE

Mid-brown and pale grey basic mice (p. 14) are all set for a formal wedding.

The tip of the bride's triangular doily veil is stuck between her ears, and silver doily makes her rose-bordered tiara. Similar roses made from ½in (10mm) squares of blue tissue (basic method 18, p. 71) form her bouquet.

The groom sports a white flower (basic method 19, p. 71) on his black tail coat. For his hat, cut two parallel slots about ⅜in (10mm) apart in a ¾in (20mm) circle of black paper: fit *base* of ears through slots – then stick to head. Roll up and stick a ⅝in (15mm) deep strip of paper for the crown, and stick between ears.

COMING AND GOING

These decorations are illustrated in colour plate 7 facing page 60

Arrivals or departures always call for a party. Bon voyage – welcome home – happy retirement – or a housewarming. And then there is the annual event of saying farewell to the old year – and ringing in the New. These wall and table decorations will help to set the scene for any such occasion.

FREIGHT TRAIN SPECIAL

A freight train to carry nuts, olives and savoury biscuits for a buffet, or sweets and lollipops at a children's party.

Use a set-square to ensure accurate corners. Or, even easier, draw each pattern on *graph paper* – and transfer it by pricking corners and ends of lines: then, following your original, join the dots.

Materials

Medium-weight coloured paper; directions
   describe the version illustrated (facing
   p. 60) – in green, yellow, pink and blue
Heavy black and grey paper (or mount on
   thin card)
Medium-weight card (eg cereal cartons)
Matchbox
Self-adhesive round black labels – also white
   and coloured (optional)
Cord or thick wool, yarn or string, to link
Cotton wool
Matt-surfaced transparent adhesive tape
Wallpaper paste
Copydex adhesive

52

Engine

1. Cut card as Fig. 59 for boiler, making a $\frac{3}{8}$in (10mm) diameter hole in the top, as indicated. Score broken lines, bend round and join side to top with tape. Bend front and back down, and tape to sides and base.

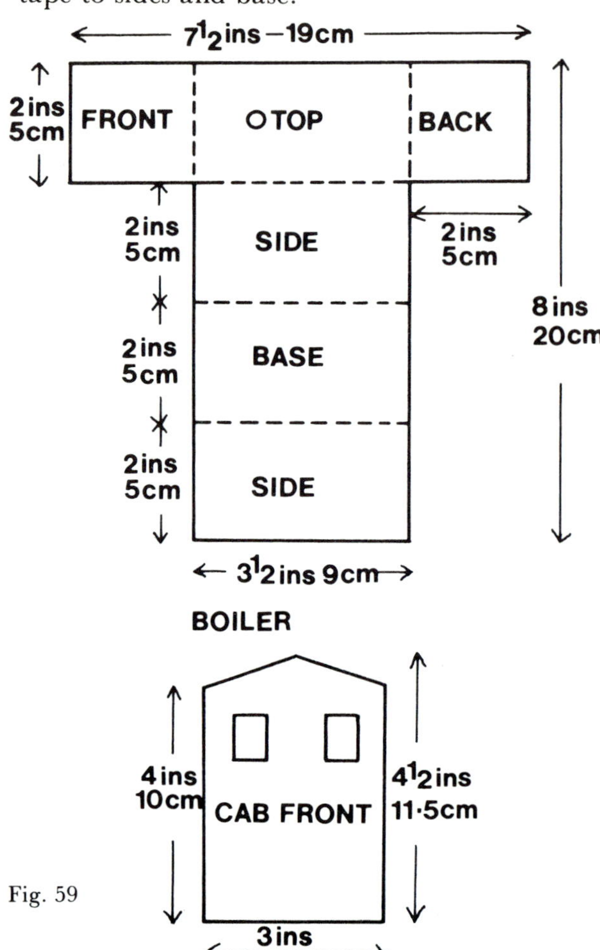

Fig. 59

Freight train special

Paste green paper smoothly over top, sides, and then front, folding neatly over edges and snipping corners. Prick a hole in paper over hole in top – then snip to edge of card all round, forming tiny tabs. Cut strips of yellow paper with pinking shears and stick over top and sides for decoration. Stick a 1½in (4cm) diameter yellow circle to boiler front, followed by smaller circles in blue, pink and black (see picture).

2. Cut cab front in card as shown. Paste blue paper over outside of front, level with edge: cut out windows. Repeat with yellow paper inside.

3. Cut a piece of card 1½ × 3in (4 × 8cm) – width × length, for roof support, and score width-ways across centre. Tape to sloping top edges of cab front.

Cut card for roof 2 × 3½in (5 × 9cm). Cover with pink paper: score centre and stick to roof support.

4. Cover matchbox with green paper.

5. Cut card for base as Fig. 60. Score broken lines: bend front down and back up. Cover inside back yellow, and outside blue.

6. Stick cab front to boiler back, lower edges level: stick matchbox to cab front to form bottom of cab. Then stick boiler, cab front and matchbox to base, sticking back section against matchbox. Cut black buffer 2½ × ¾in (6 × 2cm): stick across front.

7. Cut six dark grey wheels – two: 1¾in (45mm);

two: 1¼in (30mm) and two: 1in (25mm) in diameter. Stick to sides as shown (smallest at the back) – *so base of each wheel comes exactly ¾in (20mm) below base of engine.* Finish centres with a small black circle.

8. Draw a quarter-circle on pink paper for the smoke-stack, as Fig. 60. Draw another curve 1in (25mm) inside, as shown. Using compasses, mark outer edge ten times at ½in (12mm) intervals. With your ruler against points A and C, mark the inner curve with points D. Join points B–D as broken lines, to form five points: then join A–D to mark overlap. Cut out, cutting away shaded area at top, and also a tiny section at A, as indicated.

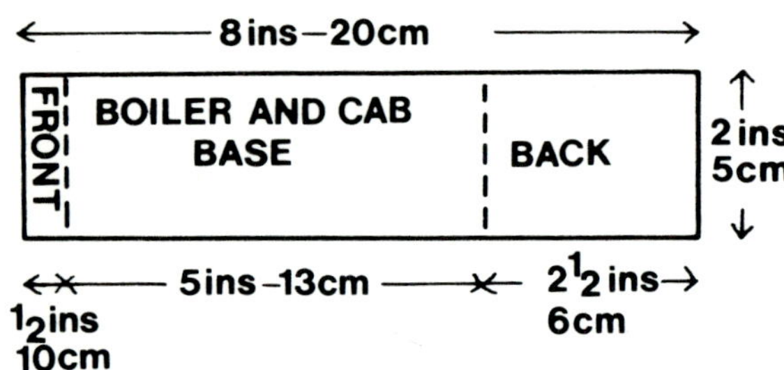

Fig. 60

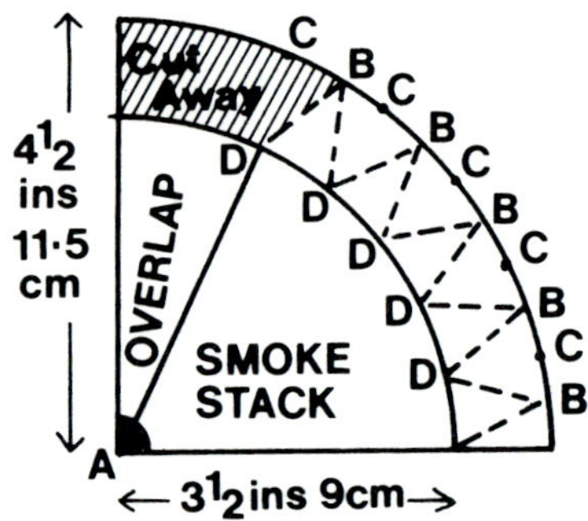

Curve round to form a cone, and stick overlap. Decorate, and curl points round, as illustrated (basic method 5 – p. 67). Stick securely into boiler.

9. Stick coloured circles on buffers, etc., and draw 'dials' on white circles to stick inside cab.

54

Tender

1. Rule card as Fig. 61, and score broken lines: with point of compasses at A, and radius 1¼in (30mm), draw a quarter-circle (B–C) on each side – then join C–C. Cut out, cutting away shaded section.

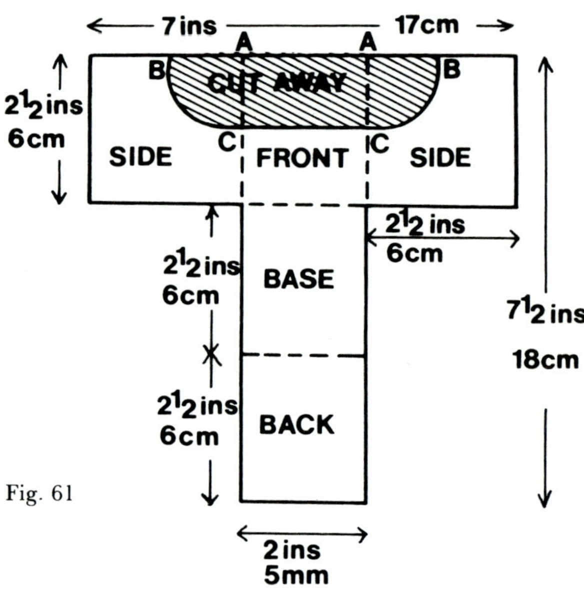

Fig. 61

2. Bend front and back up, and sides round, taping sides to back and base. Paste green paper round, trimming top edge level, and folding under base. Decorate as illustrated (facing p. 60).

3. Cut two wheels 1¼in (30mm) and 1in (25mm) in diameter, sticking to sides, and finishing, as 7 above.

Trucks

1. Cut card as Fig. 62. Score broken lines, bend up sides and ends, and tape together. Cover sides with different coloured papers, top edge level, but overlapping ends and base. Then cover ends, folding over top edge and round base. Decorate as illustrated.

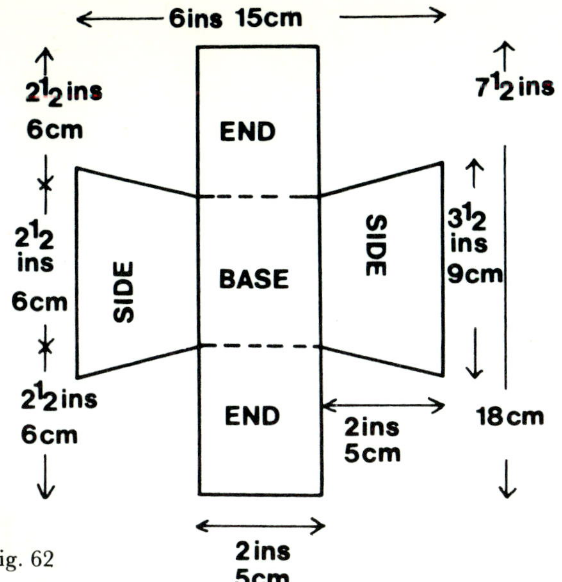

Fig. 62

2. Cut four wheels 1¼in (30mm) in diameter: stick to sides, wheel centres over corners. Finish as 7 above.

Guard's Van

1. Cut card as Fig. 63, cutting a 1½in (4cm) diameter hole in the top. Score broken lines:

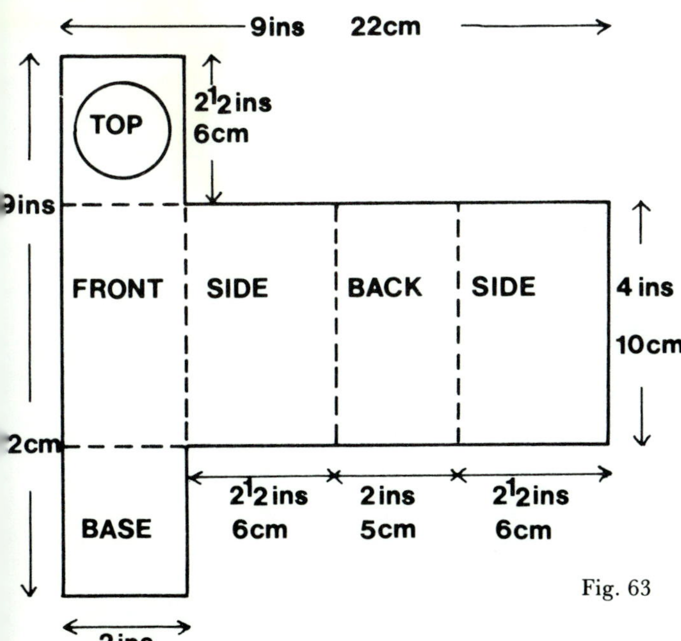

Fig. 63

bend round and tape side to front. Bend top and base over: tape to sides and back. Paste yellow paper all round, overlapping top and base: decorate sides with strips as illustrated.

2. Draw and cut out grey windows $1 \times \frac{3}{4}$in (2.5 × 2cm), and a grey door $3 \times 1\frac{5}{8}$in (8 × 4cm). Stick into place, decorating door as sides. Cut step as door, and mount on card: stick under base, protruding $\frac{5}{8}$in (3cm) at back.

3. Cut roof card $3 \times 2\frac{1}{2}$in (8 × 7cm), with a $1\frac{1}{2}$in (4cm) hole in the centre. Cover with blue paper, folding edges under (mitre corners as basic method 3 – p. 66). Cut a $\frac{3}{4}$in (2cm) circle over hole in card: snip surplus to edge of card to form tiny tabs, and stick neatly round underneath. Stick to top of van.

4. Cut four 1in (25mm) diameter wheels: fix as trucks, and finish as 7.

Make holes and link cord between each piece, securing ends inside with tape or adhesive. Push cotton wool into smoke-stack.

Load up as required. Picture shows tender filled with cut liquorice, trucks with sweets, and lollipops standing in guard's van.

NEW YEAR WISHING RING

This wreath is based on the traditional Scandinavian 'kissing bough' – hung in a porch or entrance hall to welcome guests on a cold night.

Materials

Light green and yellow (optional) face tissues
Medium-weight card
9in (23cm) diameter lampshade ring
6 glass baubles
Small curtain ring
Very fine cord to hang
Fine black sewing thread
Adhesive tape
Wallpaper paste
Copydex adhesive

1. Cut a 10in (25cm) diameter circle in card,

then cut an 8in (20cm) diameter hole in the centre. Fix the lampshade ring underneath with tape.

2. Cut strips of yellow (or green) tissue about 2in (5cm) wide. Paste thoroughly, then lift gently, fold lengthways, and wrap round card and ring – continuing until circle is completely bound (Fig. 64). Leave to dry.

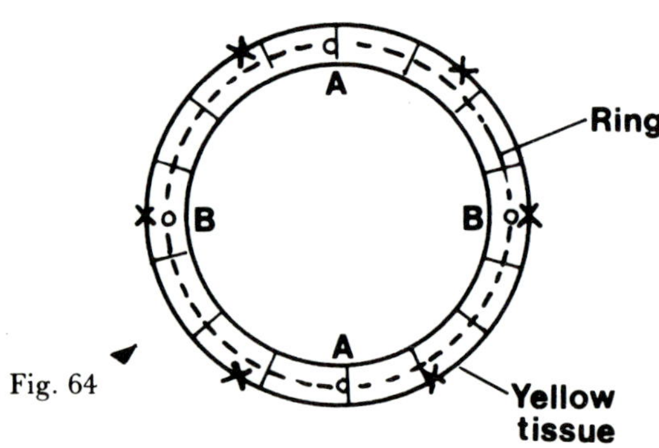

3. Cut two 18in (45cm) lengths of fine cord, and tie knots about 2in (5cm) from each end, so the distance between is identical on both. Thread one piece through the curtain ring – then fix over the circle between *o*'s A–A, tying ends through the card (taking in the ring beneath), the knots resting against the card. Repeat with second piece between *o*'s B–B – threading through curtain ring as before.

4. Fix the baubles with thread round outer edge of circle (*x*'s on Fig. 64), so they hang 2in (5cm) below the card.

5. Cut twenty-four large leaves in strengthened green tissue (basic method 7 – p. 67). Sticking the base of each leaf (shaded area) to the top of the card, and positioning as Fig. 65, arrange the leaves evenly round – one over each bauble and three between. (Cut slits for cord.)

6. Cut twenty-four small leaves and fix as shown over divisions between first ones, and close to inner edge of circle.

7. Finally, stick another twenty-four small leaves *underneath* the circle – exactly level with the smaller ones above.

56

Fig. 65

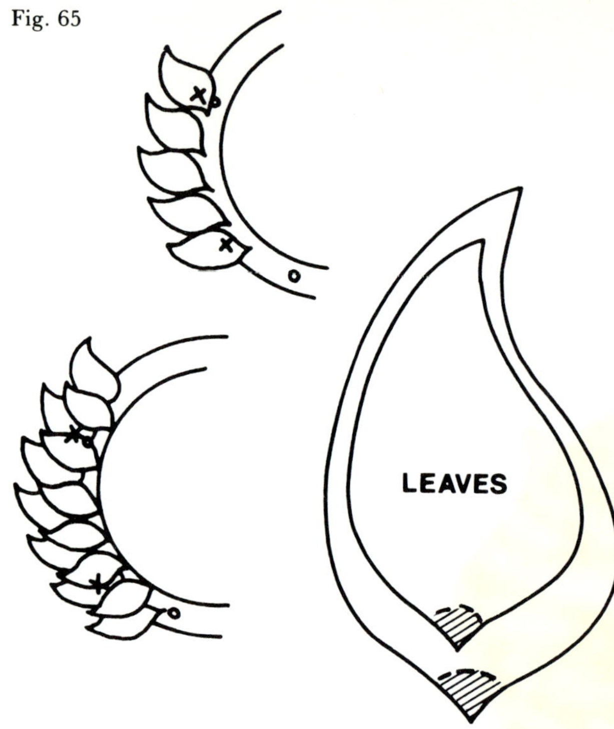

JEREMY JESTER

A mischievous little jester to join in the New Year revelry or any children's party. If you hang a small calendar from the centre point of his collar, his cheerful grin will stretch from January to December.

Materials

Blue, purple and white paper for cap, collar
  and ruff
Flesh-pink paper for face
Brown paper for hair
Medium-weight card
Kitchen foil
Silver stars (optional)
Sewing thread
Cord to hang
Adhesive tape
Copydex adhesive

1. Rule card into ¾in (2cm) squares and draw out pattern, following Fig. 66 carefully. Cut out.

EACH SQUARE = ¾ inch 20mm

Fig. 66

2. Trace the face on to pink paper (basic method 1 – p. 66). Cut out – just outside edge of circle. Trace hair only on to brown paper: cut lower edge with pinking shears – and outer edge as face. Stick to face. Draw features, in black and brown (see illustration facing p. 60).

3. Trace cap on to blue paper. Cut out inner circle – but cut *beyond* outer edge. Cut a purple collar in the same way. Cut ruff in white, following broken line.

4. Stick face in position on card. Stick cap, and then collar, round face: add ruff. Cut shape of cap and collar level with edge of card.

5. Crumple five 1½in (4cm) squares of foil into tiny balls. To fix each, thread a needle, push it through ball, cut the thread off short and tape ends behind point of cap to hang as illustrated. Decorate cap with stars.

6. Fix a loop of cord at the back, to hang.

TOURIST MOUSE

The basic mouse (p. 14) wears a warm muffler cut from the edge of a paper napkin – the ends finely fringed. His suitcase is card – 1 × 1½ × ½in (25 × 40 × 10mm) – covered with patterned paper and topped with a handle made from coloured tape.

CHRISTMAS PAST AND PRESENT

These decorations are illustrated in colour plate 8 facing page 61

Traditional songs and carols . . . and the frosty weather we associate with Christmas inspire decorations which both glisten like ice and sparkle with a warm glow of festive good cheer.

AND A PARTRIDGE IN A PEAR TREE

If, on the twelfth day of Christmas, your true love does not send you a plump round partridge in a pear tree – make your own. Experiment by mixing tissues of different colours to make your bird's plumage more striking.

Materials

Face tissues for bird (here white, blue and
   violet)
Green face tissues for tree
White (or green) face tissues to bind frame
Red, and a scrap of gold, foil paper
Black paper (or self-adhesive labels) for eyes
Thin card
7in (18cm) diameter lampshade ring
Cord to hang
Fine black sewing thread
Black ink, paint, or fibre-tip pen
Wallpaper paste
Copydex adhesive

Ring

1. Cut white tissues in half to pad ring: fold each strip lengthways *twice*. Bind ring *twice*, each twist half-overlapping the last. Stick ends of strips to hold.

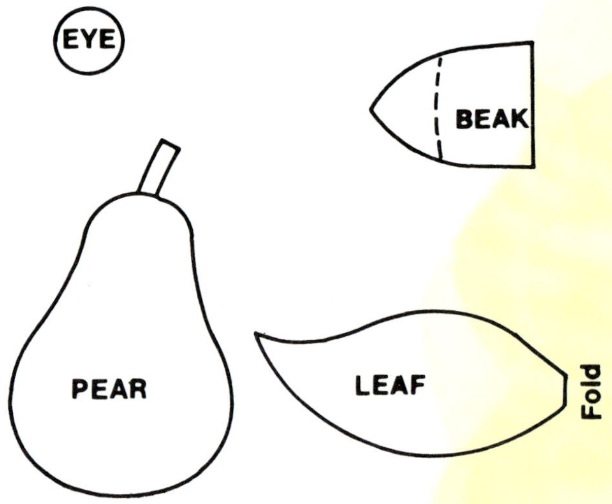

Fig. 67

2. Cut a green tissue into *four* strips. Fold each lengthways, and bind neatly over white.

3. Trace leaf and make a template (basic methods 1 and 2 – p. 66). Cut about thirty pairs of leaves in *folded* strengthened green face tissue (basic method 7 – p. 67). Twist each pair slightly, then stick round ring as illustrated, working down each side from centre top, each new pair under the previous ones. Open out final pair and stick at top.

4. Tie a loop of cord round the ring at the top, to hang.

Partridge in a pear tree

5. Make a template for the pear. Ignoring the stalk, cut eight times in red foil – reversing pattern for four. Paste to card and add card stalk. Cut out: blacken stalk. Stick between leaves as shown.

Partridge

1. Place sixteen tissues together and pin corners (these are violet, white, blue and white – repeated four times). Make a puff-ball for body. (basic method 14 – p. 70): use circles A–B–C–D–E–F–H for one half, but omit A for other half. Before sticking together, remove violet layer at back of A. Make a smaller puff-ball for head, using circles D–E–F–G–H–J – omitting D for second half. Stick balls together as illustrated, pressing head firmly against body (positioned so centres will fall behind eyes and wings).
2. Pin sixteen tissues together for wings and tail (these are alternately violet and blue). Cut and staple two single 3in (8cm) diameter puff-ball circles for the tail – and two circles E for the wings. Fold each tail circle in half, blue inside, and slightly off-centre: curve corners round towards each other and stick together at centre of fold: then stick semi-circles back to back, corners outwards. Stick to body, curving round to follow shape. Fold wing circles in half as tail, but *violet* inside – and stick to body as illustrated.
3. Cut beak in thin card, cover with gold paper, and stick between layers of head. Add black circles for the eyes.
4. Tie black thread round neck to suspend bird from top of ring.

WE THREE KINGS OF ORIENT ARE...

Tall and stately, the dignified figures of the Wise Men catch the light in their glistening, iridescent robes. The cloaks in the picture are made of silver-backed metallic foil, but kitchen foil, richly patterned with markers, makes a striking alternative.

Materials

Brown cartridge or construction paper for
   figures
Black, white and grey paper for beards,
   eyebrows and moustaches
Purple, blue and gold metallic foil or
   alternative (see above) for cloaks
Gold foil paper for crown
Cooking foil
Face tissue
Waterproof drawing inks or permanent
   markers
Transparent adhesive tape
Copydex adhesive

Figures

For each figure, cut a 6in (15cm) radius quarter-circle of brown paper. On *two* figures only, cut away a 1½in (4cm) quarter-circle at the corner. Fold in half lengthways, then open out. Fold both side edges over, to centre crease: then re-fold in half again. Cut straight between bottom corners, as broken line, Fig. 68. Open out, then overlap and stick the two outer sections – so that fold 1 becomes the front of a three-sided cone.

Fig. 68

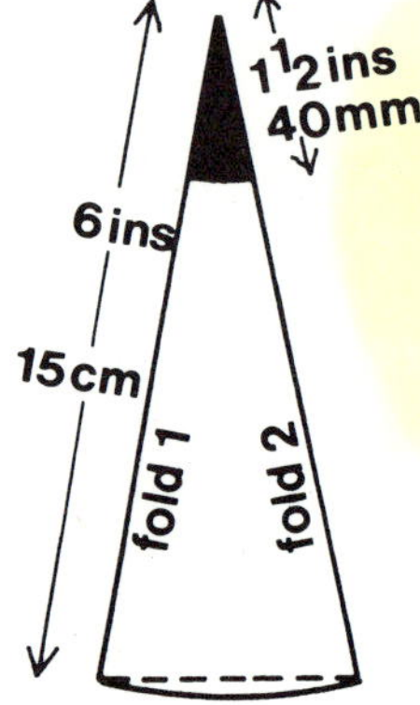

Plate 7 opposite: New Year wishing ring: Jeremy Jester: Freight train special: Tourist mouse

Three kings from the Orient

Robes

1. Cut a 6½in (16cm) radius quarter-circle of kitchen foil for each robe, cutting away a 2½in (6.5cm) radius section at the corner. Fold round figure, overlapping lower edge ½in (10mm): stick across back, and turn overlap up inside. Colour foil with inks or markers.
2. Stick a 1½in (4cm) radius quarter-circle of foil round tip of tall cone.

Pointed headdress

Cut cooking foil 4 × 2½in (10 × 6cm), and colour. Crumple surface evenly all over, then gently smooth out again. Fold lengthways into three: twist centre, then shape round cone as illustrated. Trim ends and stick.

Turban

Prepare lower section as above, and fit round top of cone. For the upper part, cut a 4in (10cm) diameter circle from a larger piece of foil prepared in the same way. Gather the edges tightly to form a ball, stuffing strips of face tissue inside to hold shape, and stick into position.

Plate 8 opposite: clockwise from top: Partridge in a pear tree and snowflakes: Three kings: Santa mouse: Snowmen

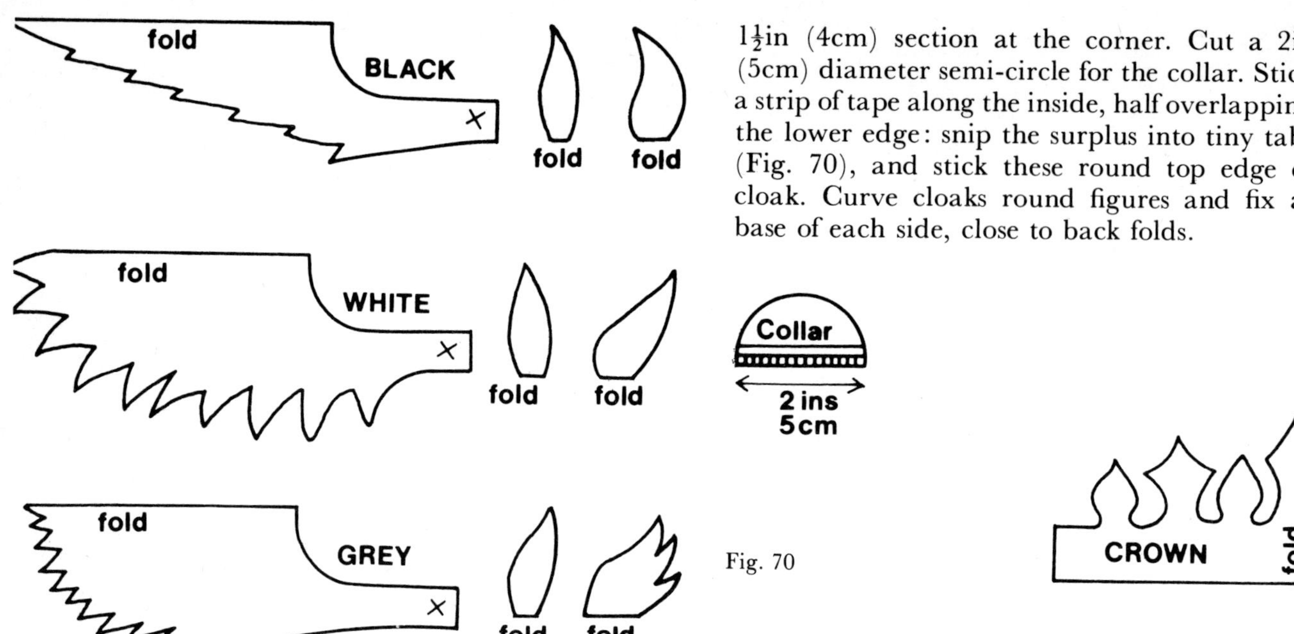

Fig. 69   Beards, eyebrows and moustaches

$1\frac{1}{2}$in (4cm) section at the corner. Cut a 2in (5cm) diameter semi-circle for the collar. Stick a strip of tape along the inside, half overlapping the lower edge: snip the surplus into tiny tabs (Fig. 70), and stick these round top edge of cloak. Curve cloaks round figures and fix at base of each side, close to back folds.

Beards, moustaches and eyebrows

Trace beards, etcetera, on to appropriate folded papers (basic method 1 – p. 66), and cut out. Stick beards to figures at *x*'s, level with cut edge of cone – or lower edge of pointed head-dress.

Crown

Prepare a circle of foil as turban, but omit tissue, and fit tightly gathered edge inside top of cone. Cut crown in gold and stick round cone.

Stick eyebrows and moustaches into place, with a little adhesive behind the centre fold.

Cloaks

Cut a 5in (12.5cm) radius quarter-circle of metallic foil (or alternative), cutting away a

SHOWER OF SNOWFLAKES

Just roll up lots of tiny balls of silver kitchen foil, pin them together – and you have made a snow-flake.

Materials

Cooking foil
1in (25mm) steel pins
Thin garden stake
Fine black sewing thread
Evo-stik clear adhesive

1. To make your first snowflake, cut out the following squares of foil:
    6 $\frac{1}{2}$in (15mm) squares
    6 $\frac{3}{4}$in (20mm) squares
    6 1in (25mm) squares
    6 1$\frac{1}{2}$in (40mm) squares
    1 2$\frac{1}{2}$in (60mm) square

Snowflakes

2. Crumple and roll each square into a ball – shiny side outside.

3. Push a pin through the centre of one of the smallest balls, followed by one each of the other sizes (in any order) – finally pushing the point into the large single ball. Repeat with five more pins (following the same order) – arranging them evenly round the large central ball (Fig. 71).

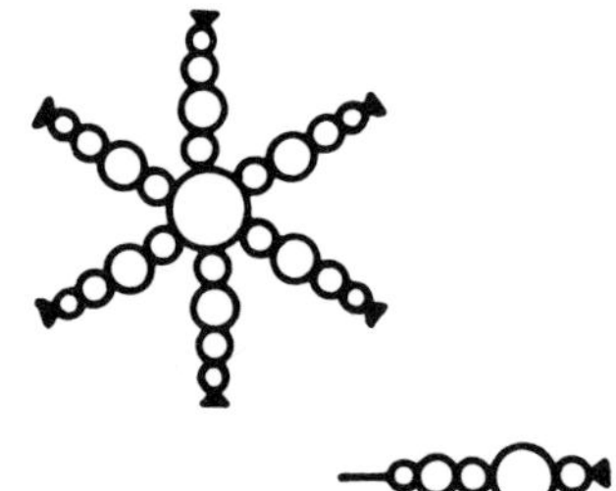

Fig. 71

4. Re-position if necessary, then one by one, draw out each pin from the central ball, coat the tip with a small blob of adhesive, and re-place in the same hole.

5. Make more snowflakes in the same way, varying the pattern by re-arranging the order of the balls on the pin, or adding one or two extra medium-sized balls as shown in Fig. 71 – or using a 3in (7.5cm) or 2in (5cm) square for the centre ball.

6. To suspend, tie black thread securely round one pin-head: then hang from the garden stake, fixing them at different heights, as shown.

ASSORTED SNOWMEN

Soft white tissues are just the right texture to simulate packed snow (best of all, use men's tissues if you have them). Their cosy 'knitted' scarves are kitchen towels – stripes added by you.

Materials

Soft white tissues (as above)

Plain or patterned coloured paper for hats, etc
Black paper for shoes
Black and red paper or adhesive labels for features
Kitchen towels
Thin card
Paper for cylinders (see below)
Felt markers, inks or water colours for scarves
Wallpaper paste (for hats – optional)
Copydex adhesive

1. Cut a 2½in (6cm) diameter circle of card, with a 1½in (4cm) hole in the centre. This is the hat brim: use it to make a cylinder (basic method 6 – p. 67), cutting waste paper about 12in (30cm) wide by required depth: these snowmen (facing p. 61) are 6in (15cm) – 5¼in (13cm) – 4½in (11cm) – 3¾in (9cm) and 3in (7cm) in height.

2. Cover both sides of brim with coloured paper. Cut a 1½in (4cm) circle of card for crown: cover one side with a 2in (5cm) circle of coloured paper, overlapping equally all round. Snip overlap to form tiny tabs, as Fig. 72. Slide brim down tube: then fit crown over end and stick tabs round top edge.

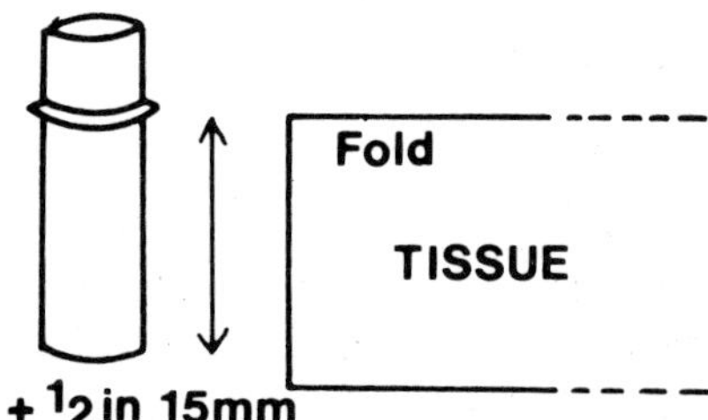

Fig. 72   + ½ in 15mm

64

3. Cut a strip of hat paper 5½in (14cm) wide by required depth – those illustrated range from 1⅝in (4cm) to ⅜in (1cm) in depth. Stick round, covering tabs. Slide brim up to meet lower edge.

4. Fold a tissue in half and cut so that depth below fold is the same as your tube from hat brim to lower edge *plus* ½in (15mm) – see Fig. 72. Stick the top corner (*x*) to fit snugly under hat brim, then wrap tissue smoothly round tube: turn cut edges under and stick. Tuck lower edge up inside tube.

5. Cut a ¾in (2cm) diameter circle of black paper in half for feet: stick in position as illustrated.

6. For the scarf, place kitchen towel on scrap paper and, working fairly quickly with markers, inks or quite wet paint, 'stripe' a panel about 1½ × 6½in (3 × 17cm) – width × length. When absolutely dry, trim edges, then cut strip up centre, making one piece slightly wider than the other. Wrap narrow strip round neck, sticking ends at front. Knot centre of other strip loosely, snip ends to form a fringe, and stick knot over ends of first piece.

7. Cut or punch circles, or use labels, for eyes, nose and buttons, following the illustration. Draw other features in black.

SANTA MOUSE

The basic mouse (p. 14) has a hat and sack made from red paper napkin. Cut the corner off a 1½in (4cm) radius quarter-circle for the hat, curve round and stick the straight edges. Trim with cotton wool. His sack is a strip of napkin 3 × 1¼in (8 × 3cm) – length × width: fold in half, stick side edges and half-fill with cotton wool before gathering and sticking top. Fluffy cotton wool makes that magnificent snowy-white beard.

BASIC METHODS AND TECHNIQUES

Here are some basic operations you will encounter whenever you work with paper – even when papering a wall! There is no need to read them all before you start – that is why they are not at the beginning of the book. Just turn to the appropriate basic method whenever the instructions for a specific design tell you to. In that way, you will be able to master each new technique as you need it. Later, when you recognise a familiar operation, you probably will not even need to refer to this section.

1. TRANSFERRING TRACINGS

Trace the pattern or design carefully. Turn the tracing over, and on the *back*, rub over all the lines with a soft lead pencil. Now turn your tracing right side up once more, place it on the surface to which you want to transfer the design, and go over the lines again – with a harder point. This will leave a clear impression, which you can draw over again to strengthen the lines, if you wish.

2. MAKING TEMPLATES – FOR PATTERNS

If you want to use a pattern often, trace it on to thin card (as above), adding any markings and identification. Cut out carefully.

3. MITRED CORNERS

To cover a piece of card with paper, cut the paper about 1in (25mm) larger than the card *all round*. Stick card to back of paper so that the overlap is equal all round (Fig. 73). Cut away each corner diagonally, as broken lines: then fold the paper smoothly over each side and stick to the back.

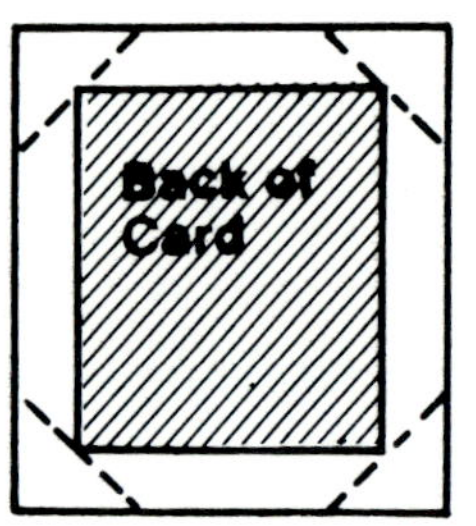

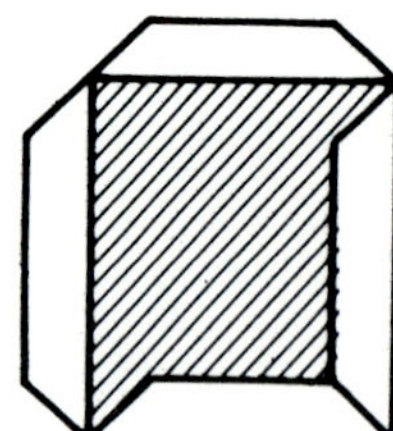

Fig. 73

4. BINDING

To bind a stem wire, pipe-cleaner or similar item: first prepare a strip of binding paper as below.

Ordinary paper: Cut a long strip the required width – usually about $\frac{3}{8}$–$\frac{1}{2}$in (10–15mm) wide.

Crêpe paper: Cut a long strip about $\frac{3}{8}$in (10mm) wide, with the grain running *across* – as arrows, Fig. 74.

Face tissue, soft napkin, etc.: Cut a strip about $\frac{3}{4}$–1in (20–25mm) wide, and fold in half lengthways: work with the fold on top – as Fig. 75.

Fig. 74　　　　　　　　Fig. 75

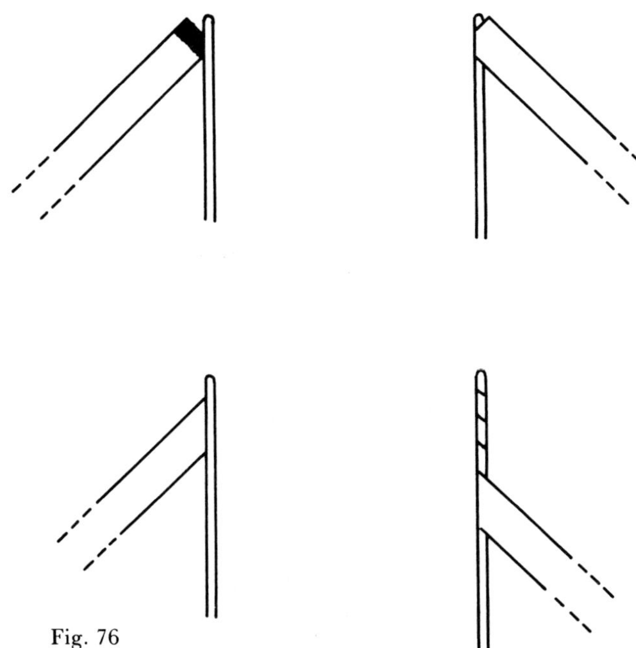

a. Smear adhesive close to cut end of strip, and press wire against lower corner, as Fig. 76.
b. Using the fingertips, and keeping the paper taut and smooth, twist strip diagonally round tip of wire as shown, continuing on down at the same angle to the bottom.
c. Cut off excess, stick end round and trim neatly.

Fig. 76

5. CURLING PAPER

Stroking: Holding the paper in one hand, and your scissors or a blunt knife in the other, draw the part to be curled firmly between the blade (on top) and your thumb (underneath), flicking off at the end.

Rolling: Roll the paper smoothly round a knitting needle or cocktail stick with the fingertips.

6. MAKING YOUR OWN CYLINDER

It is easy to make cylinders to your own measurements, so that you are not restricted to the dimensions of ready-made tubes. For instance, to make a cylinder 6in (15cm) long (or high), and 1in (25mm) in diameter, cut a piece of cartridge or construction or similar weight paper, 6 × 8in (15 × 20cm) – depth × width (the wider your paper, the sturdier your tube).

Cut a 1in (25mm) diameter hole in a piece of thin card. Roll the paper up – fairly tightly – then fit through the hole and allow it to open out so that it fits snugly inside, held by the card. Make sure the cut edges of the rolled-up paper are absolutely level at each end, then stick overlapping side edge – one half at a time, keeping the tube inside the hole while you do so. *Note:* If your cylinder will be completely covered, you can use *any* kind of smooth paper – even the thin printed pages from magazines or catalogues. Measure it as above, but cut *several* pieces the same size: use *one* to make up the cylinder, then roll the others tightly and slip them into it, so that they open up inside the tube and strengthen it.

7. STRENGTHENING TISSUES

This creates a fairly stiff piece of paper with a slightly wrinkled surface, which is particularly attractive for leaves.
a. Fold the face tissue in half: then open out again and place flat on a sheet of foil.
b. Brush wallpaper paste thickly over one half – then fold the other half over and press gently down, brushing more paste on top to ensure it is thoroughly saturated.

Leave in a warm place until absolutely dry.

8. REINFORCING TISSUES

This makes a strong piece of paper similar in appearance to the above, but thicker and flatter.

a. Cut a face tissue in half.

b. Cut a piece of light- or medium-weight paper a little larger than one piece of tissue: paste surface thickly. Press tissue down on top and brush more paste over to ensure it is thoroughly saturated.

c. When dry, cut away surplus paper, then turn over and paste second half of tissue to other side. Leave in a warm place again until dry.

9. CUTTING A SCALLOPED EDGE

a. Fold paper concertina-wise, keeping folds absolutely level.

b. Hold the paper tightly and cut scallops as required – see Fig. 77.

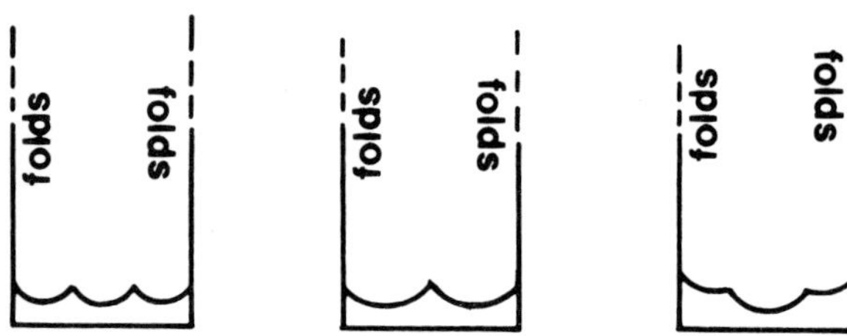

Fig. 77

c. Open up paper and smooth out folds.

10. JIG-JOG PUPPETS

Animated puppets make an amusing wall decoration, as when you pull the string, they leap into action. The bears on p. 17 are only one example: you can adapt any figure in this way. Just cut the arms and legs separately, and then join them behind the body with 2-pronged paper fasteners.

a. Trace the body once, and the arm and leg twice each (Fig. 78), on to thin card – *reversing*

your patterns for the second arm and leg. Cut out.

b. Add clothes, or other extras, as required.

c. Punch holes at large *o*'s, and pierce small holes at dots A and B at tops of arms and legs.

d. Push 2-pronged paper fasteners through holes in body and then through appropriate arms and legs. Open out prongs at back so the limbs move freely.

e. To string, fix arms with paper clips so they are just visible at sides of body – with the legs hanging straight down (Fig. 78).

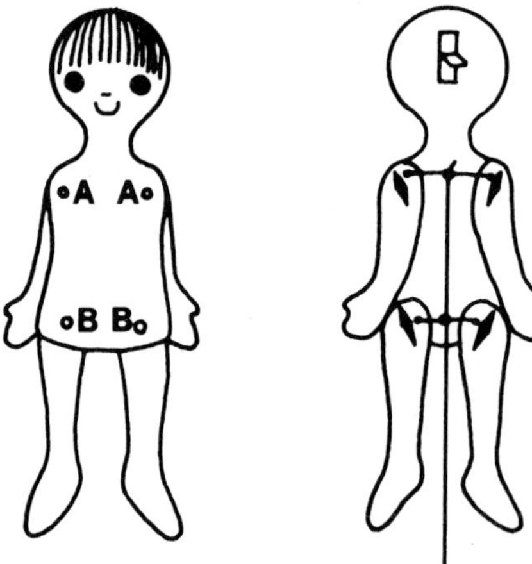

Fig. 78

f. Using strong thread or fine crochet cotton, tie tops of arms together between A–A, making sure the thread is taut. Tie the legs together between B–B in the same way.

g. Now tie a length of thread or cotton to the centre of the arm thread (A–A): attach this to centre of thread B–B – keeping it taut between as shown.

h. Trim thread at top, but leave hanging below the feet.

i. Make a small tab from a 2in (5cm) length of tape – folding it as Fig. 79 – and stick to back of head. Holding tab in one hand, pull the string with the other to animate the puppet. To hang, punch a hole in the tab.

Note: If prongs of paper fasteners are visible

from front, fix tips with tape to prevent them moving round.

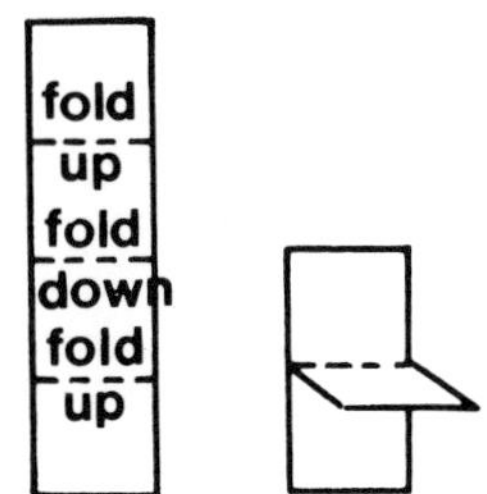

Fig. 79

11. COVERING PIPE-CLEANER ARMS

Sometimes both arms are made in one – a single pipe-cleaner stretching straight across the body, with a hand at each end (Fig. 80). Or each arm can be made from a separate pipe-cleaner, doubled in half – the bent end forming the hand (Fig. 81).

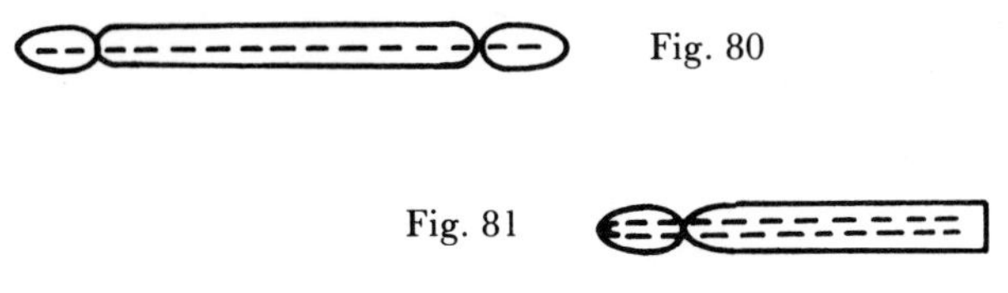

Fig. 80

Fig. 81

a. For first version, cut pink face tissue about ½in (10mm) longer than your pipe-cleaner, and 1in (25mm) deep.
b. Place pipe-cleaner along one edge of tissue (Fig. 82): roll tissue smoothly round and stick long edge neatly.

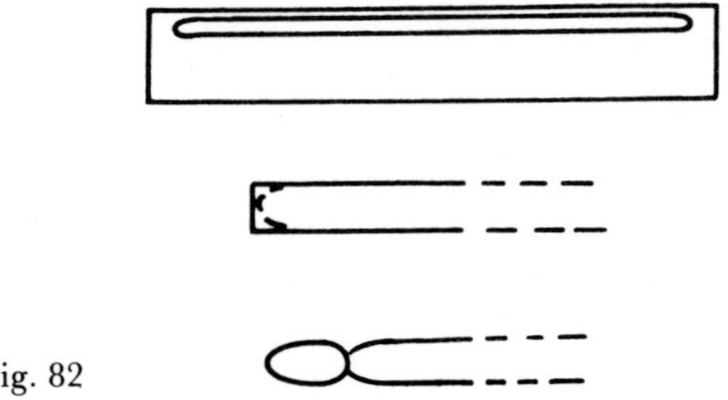

Fig. 82

c. Insert a little adhesive at each end, and pinch tissue together. Then trim an oval hand shape as shown.
d. Tie matching cotton tightly round at wrist level.

Cover a *single arm* in the same way – but make a hand at only one end, leaving tissue round *cut* ends of pipe-cleaner unfinished (Fig. 81).

12. HAIR – FROM SOFT TISSUE

Table napkins are usually best, because they come in suitable colours. But you *can* use white face tissues and paint the hair when it is dry.

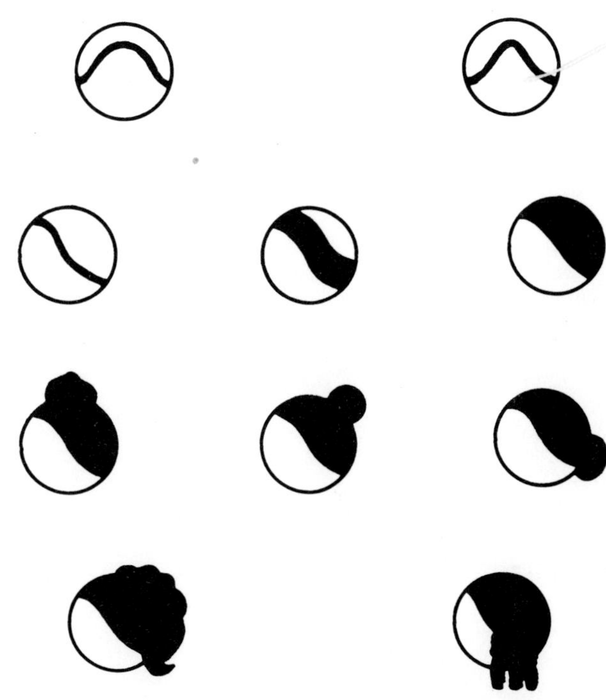

Fig. 83

a. Cut long strips of napkin roughly ½in (10mm) wide – or narrower, if working on a very small scale.
b. Brush a strip liberally with wallpaper paste and then, beginning either on top or low down at the back, wind round head to form hairline:

do not try to keep the wet paper flat – let it draw together naturally (Fig. 83).

c. Continue with more strips, behind the first one, to cover the whole head, ending at the crown. Add more strips to build up the overall shape, giving height and width.

d. Wind strips round for buns, or twist, ruche and crumple strips to form massed curls.

e. To make separate curls or ringlets, wind short pasted strips round a knitting needle or similar object, slide gently off and leave to dry on foil. Then stick into position.

13. MARKING EYES AND OTHER FEATURES

Always mark the features last. Hold the finished figure at eye level and 'visualise' where the eyes and other features should be (follow illustrations for guidance). Mark lightly in pencil, then, when you are satisfied with the expression, draw with a fibre-tip pen or drawing ink (a brown pen is good for mouths, and black for eyes).

Fig. 84

Remember that the features emphasise the character of your figure: nice, nasty, kind, bad-tempered, ugly, glamorous, charming, absent-minded, and so on. But try to keep them as simple as possible. For instance, round dots for eyes, a tiny straight line for the nose, and a small U-shaped mouth can create an amusing and mischievous personality.

14. PUFF-BALLS FROM FACE TISSUES

Face tissues, pinking shears, a mini-stapler (or needle and thread) and adhesive (Copydex) are all you need for these versatile paper balls.

Make them large or small, round or oval, by combining a selection of graduated circles from the following list. The directions for the item you are making will tell you which circles you require, identified by letters. Jot these letters down on a scrap of paper – then turn to the chart below and mark the appropriate measurement beside each.

Accuracy is important – both in measuring and cutting the circles: and then press the centre down *really firmly* each time you stick them together.

Diameter of circles

A :	2in (5cm)	H :	1⅛in (29mm)
B :	1⅞in (47mm)	I :	1in (26mm)
C :	1¾in (44mm)	J :	⅞in (23mm)
D :	1⅝in (41mm)	K :	¾in (20mm)
E :	1½in (38mm)	L :	⅝in (17mm)
F :	1⅜in (35mm)	M :	½in (14mm)
G :	1¼in (32mm)		

a. Place eight tissues together – absolutely flat – and fold in half.

b. Draw circles lightly on top of the folded tissue – about ⅜in (10mm) apart.

c. Cut round with pinking shears, inner points of notches against edge of circle.

d. Staple together at the centre (or catch tightly with thread).

e. Brush cut edges lightly with your finger to separate the layers.

f. Dab a little adhesive in the middle of the largest circle, place the next one on top – exactly central – and press the centre down *very firmly indeed, using the end of a pencil* or something similar. Repeat with the remaining circles, but press the last one down *really hard*, using the points of your small scissors or a steel knitting needle.

g. Make second half of ball, but back the largest circle with a smaller circle of thin card and check the individual instructions for any additional directions before sticking the two halves firmly together.

15. FACE TISSUE FLOWERS

a. Fold a face tissue in half – four times.
b. Draw a circle on top $\frac{1}{2}$–1in (10–25mm) in diameter. Cut with pinking shears.
c. Dab adhesive in centre of circle – then push a short pin through the middle.
d. Pinch tightly round head of pin, and fluff out layers of tissue.

16. PAPIER-MÂCHÉ ROSETTES

This versatile trimming can make a mass of tiny petals or foliage or a ruched border (see below). The points of small scissors are best for wrinkling the tissue, but a manicure or cocktail stick, knitting needle, or even a pin, would do.
a. Cut a square of tissue about twice required size. Place on foil or a flat plate and brush liberally with wallpaper paste, until thoroughly saturated.
b. Using a firm point (as above), gently push tissue up into wrinkles, working from the out-side towards the middle: poke wrinkles at centre to distribute evenly, and shape edge tidily.
c. Leave in a warm place until thoroughly dry.

17. PAPIER-MÂCHÉ RUCHING

Follow the directions above, but cut a long strip of tissue at least twice the required width, and work from outside edges towards centre. Alternatively, use tiny pieces of tissue, pushing closely together to cover an area or fill a shape.

18. PAPIER-MÂCHÉ FLOWERS

As for the rosettes, use pointed scissors, a knitting needle, manicure or cocktail stick, or a pin, to make them.
a. Cut a square of tissue to the required size: $\frac{1}{2}$in, $\frac{3}{4}$in, 1in and $1\frac{1}{4}$in (15mm, 20mm, 25mm and 30mm) squares are best – making flowers ranging from very tiny to about $\frac{3}{8}$in (10mm) in diameter.
b. Place on kitchen foil or a flat plate and brush liberally with wallpaper paste, until thoroughly saturated.
c. Using a firm point (as above), draw each corner smoothly in to the centre (as arrows – Fig. 85). Then *lift* each 'loop' (at *x* in Fig. 86), and poke it neatly down in the centre. Shape the flower evenly, finishing with a deep hollow in the centre as shown.

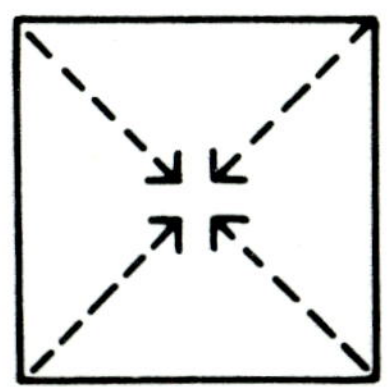

Fig. 85

Fig. 86

d. Press a pearl or bead down into the centre, if liked.
e. Leave in a warm place until absolutely dry. Then stick centre securely with clear adhesive.

19. CUT PAPER FLOWERS

a. Trace pattern **A** or **B** (overleaf) – large or small – and make a template (basic method 2 – p. 66). Use this to cut the shape in *double* medium-weight paper.

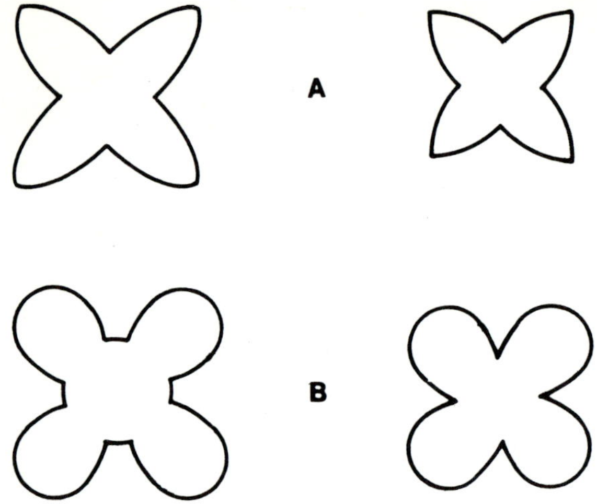

Fig. 87

20. DAISIES

a. Draw circles as shown (Fig. 88), on medium-weight paper according to the size of daisy you want. Cut round outer edge, then snip tiny petals all round, and stroke to curl them up (basic method 5 – p. 67).

b. Make a rosette (basic method 16 – p. 71) for the centre.

Note: To make a double layer of petals, stick one daisy inside another, curling the *lower* petals only very slightly.

Fig. 88

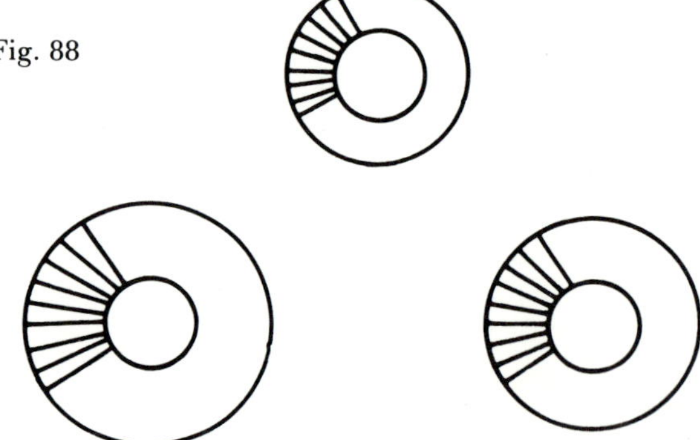

b. Stroke the petals on each piece, to curl them up (basic method 5 – p. 67). Then stick one petal shape inside the other, centres absolutely level, the upper petals falling exactly over the divisions between the petals underneath.

c. Add centres as liked.

Note: You can make a *double flower* by sticking a small one inside a large one.